GIVE FAITH A FIGHTING CHANCE

BASED ON TRUE EVENTS

Agnieszka Sycewicz

Healing Within
Tears to Success

Copyright © 2022 by Agnieszka Sycewicz

All rights reserved.

No portion of this book may be reproduced in any form without written permission from the publisher or author, except as permitted by U.S. copyright law.

Contents

Dedication	VI
Introduction	VII
1. Ilusion	1
2. Who are we?	4
3. Insecurities	7
4. Abuse!	9
5. Enough is enough	11
6. Seeking friendship	15
7. Unexpected storm	17
8. Escape	21
9. Unknown truth	25
10. Love is like a drug	28
11. Across the globe	33
12. New horizons	37
13. Awakening	42

14.	Unknown destination	46
15.	Marriage and lagos	50
16.	Try harder	57
17.	Wake-up call	63
18.	Choices	69
19.	Return of lagos	71
20.	Blinded by love	75
21.	Rebuilding from scratch	78
22.	Times of survival	85
23.	Trial of faith	87
24.	Hope for help	90
25.	Not all flowers bloom in the light	94
26.	Strangers can become best friends just as easily as best friends can become strangers	97
27.	El doctor	100
28.	Real estate	108
29.	Raising strangers	112
30.	The unexpected blessing	115
31.	"The bartender" Searching for validation	119
32.	Healing	125

33.	"El tigre"	126
34.	Lessons are repeated until they are learned	129
35.	By the time they decide to support you, they will have to book you	134
36.	Dreams turn to disaster	138
37.	Life jeopardy	141
38.	Planet collapse	143
39.	The comeback	148
40.	Back to poland	151
41.	Circle of friends	153
42.	My Hope for this Book	165
43.	Special Thank-you	169
44.	Heal Your Past	171
45.	Healing Process Exercise	180
	About the author	185

In memory of my feelings

Introduction

The life that's given to us is more than just the city or country we are born in; it is a journey and an experience that doesn't necessarily lead us to a place or home.

The lives we've each been given are road maps that have the ability to go around the entire globe, but only if we choose to follow the path and take the first steps.

Overall, life is a vision we create in our minds, and it often leads us to moments where we feel the illusion of non-existence. The unique journey each of us is on will take us places we could never imagine being part of our story. It will show us that if we have a little courage in ourselves and a little faith that the path *is* indeed there for us, the road we take doesn't have to have an end.

Over time, we will learn to take the first steps toward our destiny. Over time, we will learn that even when seemingly insignificant events seem forgotten, when broken relationships seem mended, when there's no way we can possibly hold everything in our minds at once, everything that makes us who we are is forever written into the story of our lives.

My hope is that your journey through my story will help you recognize how your choices and past experiences have shaped the life you lead today. I hope reading how I got to the place I am today allows you to see that life is about falling and getting back up, not always knowing why circumstances occur but believing in the process. I truly believe that after reading this book, you will feel compelled to *Give Faith a Fighting Chance.*

"The greatest glory in living lies not in never falling, but in rising every time we fall." - Nelson Mandela

Chapter 1

Ilusion

"The road to recovery is a long and often painful journey."

Most people live their lives amongst beautiful lies, only to find out later that they were in the midst of some of the biggest illusions humankind has to offer.

I was born in Poland, into circumstances and a city in which people's dreams were not so easily achieved. My family was one of extreme poverty, with layers of alcoholism and non-working parents. The beginnings of my life were not what anyone would have asked for if they had a say..

When we hear these kinds of stories, we can all think of how we relate in some way. It's part of human connection - we look for similarities. Maybe you didn't grow up with the circumstances I did, but you might be able to look back on your own childhood and wonder: What were your dreams? What did you want for yourself? What was your view of the world at that time, and how was it shaped by what surrounded you? Many times, we use looking back on our childhood as a way to piece together what made us who we are now. Some people might pinpoint moments in childhood that gave them grit, determination, drive. Yet others might reflect back and blame their childhood for how it shaped or traumatized them, how it led to unhelpful habits or behavior patterns that made it harder - maybe even "impossible" - to achieve success.

As a little girl with no guidance, mentors, or direction, I saw nothing to look forward to. There was constant abuse in my house and a distorted view of what life should look like; dreams and goals were not something I even understood, let alone created for myself. To young me, life just was what it was. You got what you got, and there was no way to make change.

As I grew to be a teenager, I still lacked a supportive familial structure - really, any structure - in my life. I was always the black sheep in my household. Regardless of what decisions anyone else was making at home, I was constantly reminded by my parents and family members that I would never amount to anything, that I'd be in jail or dead before I knew it. This reinforcement of negative beliefs became my reality, as my teenage "years" turned into adulthood almost immediately.

Because of the life I had at home, I began looking for escapes from the cards I had been dealt. Along with the treatment I was given by my parents, I also saw how the world treated my parents, and these experiences, I had very little hope for adopting a different outlook on what existence could be. This might seem different from other stories, when people talk about their undesirable circumstances leading them to want better or more for themselves. For some reason, this wasn't me.

Unfortunately, the "escape" I imagined in my head was not what I truly needed in my life. When I was 12, I desperately began searching for a way out of my reality at home, only to find myself plummeting downhill toward exactly the same, if not a worse fate than the one I was already trying to run away from.

I started smoking, using drugs and alcohol to take me away from my life. When I say I was using drugs, I'm talking about every single drug choice that existed on the face of the earth. All these choices put me precisely into the wrong environments, in the wrong places and with the wrong people, at such an early age. This wasn't the way out, but it seemed like the only option. No one starts using drugs thinking they will become addicted.

Chapter 2

Who are we?

"Other people's opinions of you don't have to become your reality." - Les Brown

The titles that are given to us often form our perceptions of who we think we are.

My older sister left home at 15 years old to seek a better life, which meant that pretty early on, I was all alone. I can't necessarily say my parents didn't care, but they didn't know *how* to care in the way they needed to. My sister was always the example to strive toward in my family. Very different from me as I was often reminded, she was a good student and very smart in every aspect - she knew how and when to be polite, and how to properly eat, drink, sit, dress, and talk. Everyone who knew her was always proud of her. She was the only one in the family who didn't even think of dropping out of high school. My sister met a guy who was a little older than her, and he came from a very stable and wealthy family. She found a guide in his mother, who took her in as her own daughter. She was cared for there, given a life that could prepare her for the future she wanted. She spent more than eight years with him and his family. Every time she'd come to visit, which was quite often, she always cared to bring whatever she could to our house, to give a helping hand.

During this time, even though she was living away, I was the one who was truly absent. I watched my sister become so perfect in everything she did, and it was just another reminder of what a disaster I was in comparison. She eventually went on to college, making the time she spent away from us worth something. I never tried to hate the fact that she was walking perfection in everyone's eyes, but I got used to believing I exemplified the title I was given - the Big Mess. The girl who didn't know how to hold a fork or knife, the girl who never knew how to be polite or how to properly eat, drink, sit, dress, or talk. I was the girl who repeated a grade over and over again, and greeted life with no common sense. To everyone around me, and thus, to myself, I was not smart at all.

Throughout all of this, I was always trying to understand what was wrong with me. I had no natural "ambition" at all. All I did was blame the choices I was making - the ones that brought me closer to darkness and away from the light - on how I had been raised. My sister didn't do this; all of her decisions were always seemingly aimed for the good anyway. I guess she was born with that power, or saved by leaving home, just in time to be raised differently than I was. Even though we came from the same home, even though we are family, we didn't get to know each other very well, especially after she moved. To me, she is what everyone always said she was: perfect. I'm the opposite. In my family's eyes, no matter what I accomplished, I was always seen as who I "used to be." The problem came when I believed that's all I ever could be.

Chapter 3

Insecurities

"We are the only ones who can create our own reality." - Agnieszka Sycewicz

Our time in school is a critical time for developing our sense of self, and it's a time many children want to remember forever. Especially for those of us who experienced unstable home lives, school could serve as a kind of escape.

For me, school was another kind of hell. I struggled with insecurities and bullying, which was the cherry on top of my formative teenage years and only added to what I had going on back home. Being picked on and laughed at by other kids made every day a dark one. I stopped wanting to communicate with others, even though I wanted so desperately to be liked. Instead of finding other people to hang out with, I became best friends with my own shadow.

I found myself sitting against the walls alone, talking to myself, going through what was wrong with me that made everyone dislike me so much. Through this, already present insecurities magnified, which is something that continued to haunt me for a large part of my life.

I wasn't very popular or pretty compared to the other girls, which furthered my anxiety around being liked by others. The girls in my classes wanted nothing to do with me. They all gathered in groups while I lingered back, against the wall staring at them and wishing I could be their friend. Over time, I slowly started becoming a girl who wanted to hang out with the guys more than the mean girls who were making my life impossible. I didn't really care anymore anyways, I was already labeled as the mess. I began shifting my appearance to adopt a more "manly" persona, dressing up in baggy pants with hats, chains, and big shirts that I begged to borrow from my fat neighbor since we couldn't even afford a new book bag in my house. I switched my identity completely, trying to cover up my true self and insecurities with baggy clothing.

The next thing you know, I was holding a skateboard in my hand and found myself a part of a skater's gang, being the only girl on the team. I guess, looking back, this was the beginning of me trying to find some self-esteem, gaining back what I had been losing while I grew older. It felt rewarding, because every time I was able to prove I could be as good as them, I was validated by them and able to develop some confidence. With this new identity, I was no longer afraid to be laughed at or bullied by anyone in school.

Chapter 4

Abuse!

"I felt so much pain that I started to feel nothing." - Unknown

Witnessing the abuse and instability between my parents left a wound that I carried for a long time without consciously knowing it marked the beginning of my mental breakdowns and lack of growth as a person. Both my mother and father nearly lost their lives over each other's stupidity, with drunken moments, constant fights, and verbal and physical disrespect. Being a child, I had no idea what I could do to stop the madness around me, but I also grew to think of my parents' relationship as normal.

Some of us take a lifetime to recover from traumatic events or periods of our childhood. Some of us block out our traumas, which can feel good for a bit but leads to us not revisiting them or finding ways to recover from them at all. When you find yourself living in the midst of any type of abuse, mental instability, fear, or insecurity, you don't see a path to healing in your present moment.

You start on a downward spiral, believably coming to the realization that nothing is worth living for. That's what happened to me as I grew into a young woman with seemingly "no feelings" or reactions toward pain. As it became more prominent in my life, I started to become less afraid of darkness. Suffering didn't seem as bad anymore. I no longer felt any fear; the feelings of loneliness and struggle were slowly going numb, leaving behind a sense of courage that I didn't know I could possess.

Chapter 5

Enough is enough

"When you're afraid of the unknown and still stand up for yourself, that's when you realize you can stop the suffering."

As I go deeper into my past, trying to explain myself and all the different reasons for my actions, I honestly cannot find answers. The only thing I can say is that there came a point where I started becoming fearless.

I truly believe this can be a blessing and a curse at the same time.

As my story continues, this newfound courage meant that I would no longer allow scenes of violence on my watch or in my presence, especially not in the place I called "home."

The problem was that I didn't know what to do to stop it. How could I, a child, stop the beatings from my parents or anxious emotions I felt every time I walked into my own house?

I remember this next event as if it were yesterday. One evening when I came home, it was immediately apparent that my dad was so mad, so drunk, and so unstable. The moment I walked in I could already see what was coming for me, but the hitting and fighting started sooner than I thought. Quickly I found myself being pushed into the closet, screaming for help and shouting as loud as I could, "Stop! Stop!" without any control or ability to defend myself.

Then, all of a sudden, I became this completely different person, the one I had felt brewing inside me for some time. With every ounce of strength I had, I started fighting back like I was a fighter in a boxing ring. I pushed my dad away and started beating him back, losing control of my own behavior, almost as if a demon was coming out of me.

As I hit him I yelled out loud, "If you ever touch me again, you will never see another light in your life!" Even though I felt sheer terror in the moment, I also remember feeling so much adrenaline. Not a tear came out of my eyes.

As the fight continued between us, all I could see out of the corner of my eyes was my mom and sister, both in tears, trying to stop the awful situation. To be honest, I think they were more afraid of what would happen to me after the fight ended. Though I'm sure they tried, they couldn't separate the angry, fearless demon that was coming out from who I truly was.

Staring at their faces as I threw punches left and right toward my dad, I got myself out of the fight and started running away to get help. I begged a neighbor to let me use her phone. As exacerbated as I sounded, I called the police and made the whole thing out to be even bigger than it really was.

I wasn't sure exactly what I was doing as I made the phone call, but I knew this had to have an end.

Minutes later, my dad was handcuffed and put in jail for child abuse. At the time, I didn't really understand yet what made this incredible courage come to life; all I could see was an end to all the suffering I had endured in the past.

Honestly, I still don't have an explanation of what made that day the end in my mind. Maybe I was just tired and had finally had enough, maybe there was too much hate and resentment inside me for growing up with so much pain. Maybe the numbness simply overtook my sense of fear that day.

I felt like an unstoppable victor, but when I got back home and saw the look on my mother's face, I realized the care and love I always hoped to receive from her was never coming in the way I wanted. In her eyes I saw what a horrible daughter she thought I was, to be capable of hurting my father in the way I did.

To her, there was never a question as to why I was being beaten, the big picture remained - somehow even bigger - that I was the devil. But my emotions were so deeply buried already. I knew in the depths of my heart, despite how the numerous negative titles I was given, that I had something within that was so scary, so strong. It was the drive and ability to stand up for myself. That in and of itself was my rebirth. I was becoming the person I am today. No matter how I viewed myself, my family hated me for engaging in the fight and for calling the police on my father for a long time.

After my father got out of jail, I overthought every possibility. What was going to happen to me now that he was back? Was

I afraid? I decided I was not! And after this point, no one ever threatened me again. I was a 13-year-old girl who, in searching desperately for help, found the most safety within herself.

During the next couple of days, everything was relatively quiet and peaceful like never before. The noises of the past subsided and allowed room for the voices inside to start. Guilt was taking over, which was a new feeling for me. Until this point, I had never cared about or felt guilt for anything I had done. My strength all of a sudden had a shadow behind it.

The experience took some pain away from me, and what lingered was regret - mixed with a sense of peace unlike any other. The peace I finally created for myself wasn't enough to keep me relieved for long. I started asking myself, "Did the need for escape really serve as the reason for my actions?"

Maybe throughout all of this, I just wanted a reason for someone to punish me.

Chapter 6

Seeking friendship

"Never forgotten: Hope."

We all seek out that one best friend - the person we can share our lives with and feel completely comfortable displaying our true selves. For me, her name was Hope. I think she was truly my very first "best girl friend" and our friendship lasted many, many years of my adolescence. We were two crazy teenagers, always together. Though we came from very different families and backgrounds, we managed to find each other for the best and worst times in our lives.

We hadn't gotten too far along in our friendship before we started to get into trouble. We started going out every night, dropped out of school, started stealing and doing drugs... I mean the *worst* possible behaviors for two kids. God knows how many memories we share with one another which lead to me being arrested at the age of 13 and being sent to jail.

Of course, punishment from law enforcement never taught me much of a lesson at all.

Everything for us was just fantasy, fun, an illusion. Reality didn't really exist for me at that time. Hope was my only friend there with me - the only girl friend I ever had - and I wasn't going to lose that friendship for anything. Our crazy lives continued, and we got so close that we experienced all of our formative "firsts" together. All we had was each other, despite adults in our lives wanting us to stop spending time together. Even though it was not the most healthy friendship - much of the time we were unconscious, on drugs, creating a reality that was more blurry than you could ever imagine - it was the very first one that showed me what it feels like to be wanted, happy, and free. Even though Hope and I, as we got older, chose different paths for our lives and went our separate ways, I can confidently say she was the only woman I truly loved at that point in my life. Our friendship is one of the best memories from my teenage years.

Chapter 7

Unexpected Storm

"The hard times I have been through taught me that those moments don't last forever, but the toughness you find within you because of them does!"

Traumatic events in our lives can make us wonder if we made the right choices. We ponder whether, if we had thought or acted only slightly differently, the event would have still happened or the outcome would have been the same. Sometimes though, it's important to know that life isn't 100% in our control, and things happen without our permission or desire. In these cases, healing and moving forward are the only aspects over which we have a say.

This next event was not a choice I made, something I could not predict or control. And the moment it occurred in my life, it changed me forever.

One early, cold, snowy morning as I was walking to school, a shadow behind a tall tree entered my peripheral vision amidst the sea of white surroundings.

As I started moving toward a small bridge that crossed the frozen lake, I kept my eye on the tree, becoming increasingly more apprehensive. I knew something wasn't right. Looking back on this moment I sometimes catch myself thinking, Why didn't I turn around? Why didn't I stop in my tracks? Why didn't I go back home? I was just a kid, but occasionally I still tell myself I should have known better.

Terrified, I kept walking, and out from behind the tree came the shadow that I had previously seen. It was a big, tall man who jumped at me, almost as if he had been waiting for precisely this moment. Before I could register what was happening, he attacked me, throwing my body onto the cold and wet ground that was covered in snow. I thought he might have been a thief, but what would someone look to steal from a child with only a bookbag on them as they walked to school?

Soon, I could feel the inches of snow beneath me begin to melt as the man breathed heavily on top of me. His strong hands wandered across my body, tearing my clothes, and I knew it was time to fear for my life. Instead though, my mind went blank. It felt empty as instincts took over. While it seemed nearly impossible to get the man off of me, I fought. Luckily, I had style at this time, and I was wearing platform shoes that were as thick as they could get. I used them as my weapon, kicking at him with every ounce of strength I possessed. By the grace of God, I was able to get out from underneath him, escape the attack, and run as fast as my feet would take me to get help.

I found help; soon, strangers were calling the police and carrying me into a school behind the gates of the lake. I had to talk to the police, then there was a search for the man who attacked me. They eventually found him, and he was placed in temporary holding. Shortly after, I came face to face with him - in a cell where there was no one-way glass to protect me. As I was pressing charges, I found out he was an ex-police officer. Voices around me told me to let it go, or that he would come back for me. Still other voices called "Nothing really happened!" I felt alone. But I also felt angry. Fear was nowhere to be found inside me, no matter what other people tried to make me think.

I continued to use that path to walk to school. People gave me alternative ways, ways that would probably have been much safer or less triggering, but instead I just always looked over my shoulder. Why? I'm not sure. Maybe it was stubbornness, maybe it was the notion that I wasn't going to let that big man couldn't take anything from me. Maybe it was the need to revisit the trauma and rethink my choices. Maybe it was that I felt I deserved to have it happen again.

I used that path every day, and despite everyone knowing what had happened to me, I continued to always walk alone. I walked across the frozen lake - which was always on the brink of collapse - maybe not only to remember the dark memory of my own past, but also to bear witness to the many normalized deaths, crimes, and other tragedies that occurred in the area. People wondered how I could have no fear, how I could think what had happened to me was not a "big deal." I think the numbness had just taken over.

I still wonder why I had to land on the edge of rape - how that event became necessary in the overall story of my life. I fought my way out of a brutal and terrible experience, but I know it could have just as easily - maybe even more easily - resulted in a terrifying alternative.

Chapter 8

Escape

We all make decisions in life that, looking back, we might have changed.

Why do we do that to ourselves - make the "wrong" choice - when we know what "should" and "shouldn't" be? The answer is simple. We want to be seen! We want to be heard!

The big decision of mine that falls into this category is the one I made when I was 14 years old. I chose to leave school.

The chapters of my life till now had put me in the life period of acting out even more and all events that took place till now had no influence on me making better choices for my life.

I began to drift in the wrong direction. Memories of numbing myself with drugs and alcohol come flooding back - cocaine, amphetamine - you name it, I did it all. I was an addict, trying to kill the pain I was experiencing.

I felt mostly unconscious during my years in Poland; the only goal in my mind was to no longer exist. Even though things had always "worked out," I didn't see happiness. I couldn't seem to find anything that made living worth it. I wanted the drugs to kill me, but no matter how many times I nearly overdosed, I remained alive.

Desperately searching for a friend to talk to, I opened an empty journal in 1995 and began writing. This is where my writing journey began; I started writing poems to myself. Some of them I still have to this day, about pain, suffering, devastation, loneliness, and feeling lost.

October 25, 1995

What would I do without you, my precious, empty pages?

You are my best friends, things I can trust, because I'm certain no real person will ever hear my story.

Why didn't I talk to you before, instead of always keeping my thoughts to myself?

I know now that I no longer have to carry the heavy pieces of life in my head.

I no longer have to keep secrets to myself or hold the pain that weighs me down.

I can share what troubles me, I can talk to you out loud and you will hear my voice.

When I fill you up with stories of mine and you can't speak back to me, know that these empty pages will never be the same!

- Agnieszka Sycewicz

Writing in my journal marked the beginning of creating my own reality, making life what I wanted it to be. It was another form of escape for my pain, it became almost like another drug. I got a high each time I turned to the next page and saw that I could start over again.

Revisiting those pages and looking back on them now allows me to see that my actions were signs of a lost child searching for help, but it was help I would never find in a person no matter where I looked.

June 16, 1996

"Invisible"
    You no longer have to be "no one."
    You can choose your own top of the mountain.
    You can climb to the very top, and along the way you will meet someone who doesn't understand why you choose to keep going.
    You will meet others on that same path who will try to make you believe that the top is too steep, the mountain is too big, and the climb is too dangerous, just so you can remain the same!

- Agnieszka Sycewicz

November 23, 1995

"Freedom"
    Why can't we all accept who we are?
    Why can't we all be worthy of ourselves?

Life can be beautiful, but only for the unknown.

It's often full of pain and suffering for all humankind.

Is that fair? In what way are we capable of taking another's peace for ourselves?

People can take away your worth and take your freedom along with it, a freedom God created us to have....

How is that fair?

- Agnieszka Sycewicz

CHAPTER 9

UNKNOWN TRUTH

"People often say we need to learn to let go of the life we planned and choose the life that is given to us." I disagree!

I didn't capture the truth of my family's situation until I got older. Thinking back now, I remember anger, abuse, instability, and confusion about what love should look like, yes, but I also remember my mom disappearing in the middle of the night, and us waking up the next morning like nothing happened. I remember sometimes having the most expensive food imaginable one day, then having no food at all the next. I remember not having hot water for showers, and having electricity intermittently, needing to light candles when our power got shut off. I remember ending up homeless, with nowhere to go.

None of this made any sense to me, until the day it did. I remember seeing a man who barely spoke our language come into our home. He was dressed in a suit and carried a bucket full of roses, gifts, including bikes we could never have even dreamed of, and sweets. He stood in the door as my dad was making dinner and said, "Hello!" As I watched what was happening, I saw my mom standing next to the man with the biggest smile. They looked at my dad and started, "Now you listen, and listen carefully..." My mom began explaining to my dad the reason for this man's visit, and he handed my dad an envelope full of money. My father's eyes were full of tears. He begged the man and my mom not to leave him, but he knew with just one look that he could not compete with a man of such caliber. He had nothing to offer my mom, or us for that matter.

My father was an unemployed alcoholic with no plans of changing. All he had to give was his love and care, of which he gave the best he could. That day was the first one where I developed the biggest compassion for my dad. I could feel the pain he was going through. Yet simultaneously, I prayed my mom would walk away from him. None of this was understandable to me; all I knew was that I wanted to be out of the misery we had been living in.

The arguments ramped up about finances, love, family, and kids, and it was the most confusing debate I ever heard. How could I, at such a young age, begin to fathom seeing my father in tears, begging another man not to take his wife?

Without any explanation to us of who this man was, my mom continued on with her decision. We went looking that same day for the dream home we had been offered by the man - if only she would walk away from her marriage to my father. My mother had always been brave; she knew how to turn things around for us.

But she simply couldn't do it, I guess. The very next day, we were back with my dad living the same life we always had. The ups and downs continued, and the typical stories repeated themselves over and over. I tried to understand her reasons, but I just couldn't.

We are all given the chance to make a better life for ourselves and our families at some point, even if it is scary or doesn't make a whole lot of sense. Yet she didn't choose that better life, and once again, I was left unbalanced.

Chapter 10

Love is Like a Drug

"Love is meant to be earned, not bought." - Agnieszka Sycewicz

First love.

As my desperation for escape became more real than ever, I found myself once again picking up my skateboard and rejoining the skating gang. It had been some time, but that group was still a place I could go back to.

The skaters made a place where I could shine and experience the glory of being *good* at something, of winning.

I mean, I was good. Skateboarding was the only thing that brought light in my life; I spent days and nights practicing. When I was skating or rollerblading, I was having the best time of my day.

Anyway, I got back to skating. When I did, it didn't take long to find him. He was every girl's dream - tall, handsome, with beautiful green eyes - he was like a model. And he was newly joining our group.

His name was Tim, and looking at him was like looking at God. It was like being close to him could only ever be a dream. I was sure I had fallen in love from the first time I laid my eyes on him.

I can honestly say that I didn't really know what love was until I met Tim. But of course, as my luck goes, he wasn't single. To make matters worse, I believed at the time that my looks couldn't compete with those of any other girl.

We became friends over time, rollerbladed as partners, skated on the same team. Long hours of practicing became an excuse to get closer to one another. My feelings only grew stronger over time, muddled only by my insecurities.Matter of time he walked away from his relationship and broke up with his girlfriend. Life has a way of giving you what you want, even if it doesn't end up being right for you in the end. We started off as friends and skating partners, but unexpectedly, we did indeed become more. My dreams became a reality; we had a love story I never thought would end. To me, Tim was the last stop, the man I was going to marry.

He seemed like the light I needed, the light I had been seeking for so long. In this way, I was blinded by the love I had for him. As months, and eventually years passed, he continued to amaze me, but slowly he transformed into a man that no longer fit every girl's dreams.

There was lying. There was cheating and betrayal. Twisted events took place that mirrored my own parents' relationship, events which were plagued with disrespect for one another. What seemed like a situation that was once only filled with light turned into darkness. The blame I put on my mom for her actions and for staying with my dad came back to haunt me, as I fulfilled her position in my relationship. Breaking the cycle I had grown up with was proving to be harder than I thought.

I saw the red flags and the toxicity fairly early on, but I was so happy at the idea of being loved and wanted that I turned a blind eye to all that told me to stop. I was so afraid at the idea of being left alone and feeling unwanted once again.

Unfortunately though, all I saw in my future was more darkness. Tim's light was quickly dimming, and mine was disappearing along with it. It was only a matter of time before I lost him completely, and I couldn't bear that reality. I put all my focus into saving us, no matter what it cost me. I wanted so badly to reverse the tough times we were having, to get back to when everything was good and bright. The problem was, there was nothing I could offer him where I was, and nothing I could think of to change that. Unless...

An idea lit up in my head. I would call my uncle, who was living in the United States. He was the husband of my dad's sister, and maybe the only person I could think of who could help me.

My aunt and I were never close. She and my uncle had lived overseas since they got married, and they had been married over 30 years. They had no children, but I remember they helped my parents any time they could during their many times of crisis.

I thought it would be worth it to ask them for help, for a little getaway vacation to the States. I was quite skilled at convincing people of things I wanted from a very young age. Now, I know where it comes from! After I talked with them, I planned a whole script in my head, the plan of how exactly I was going to make Tim love me again. How desperately I wanted to feel loved again.

What I was hoping for was to come back to him with all the gifts I could possibly imagine. This would surely prove my love to him... I mean, really. Looking back now, what a plan! As I'm writing this chapter, I'm laughing at what was going through my brain during that time.

I learned, over time, not to repeat the naivete, but instead to always pay close attention to the small voices we all have deep down and follow them no matter how insane they may seem at the time.

What started out as naivete ended up changing my life forever.

In the end, going to the U.S. was the plan, the last option I believed could make my relationship with Tim right again.

My aunt wasn't convinced that I should enter her household, as she knew I wasn't exactly your average 16-year-old. She knew I was a troublemaker, and she was weary of me. However, my uncle stood up for me like no one else ever has. My aunt finally said "yes," but only if I brought my sister along with me. Shortly after, we both applied for our visas and underwent the interview and questioning process. In the end, I was granted a six-month visa while my sister's application was denied. How and why this happened, I will never know.

The next day, my uncle bought my ticket. I was excited, full of hope and happiness. As I gathered my belongings and said goodbye to Tim, he handed me a list of items he wanted me to bring back.

To me, this was just the beginning of our everlasting love. I wanted so badly to have something to offer. With that, I was off.

Chapter 11

Across the Globe

"If we can only turn our denial into acceptance sooner than we do, the lasting confusion that stays with us for the longest of times will turn into clarity faster than we ever imagined!"

As I arrived in the U.S. for the first time, everything was like a dream. The people, the places, the food, the views... Wow. I thought to myself that it was finally one reality I didn't want to escape. It was a dream come true that I never knew I had. I remember being in the airport and, for the very first time in my whole life, men stared at me as if I was from another planet. It was a powerful feeling; I had never gotten so much attention in all my time in Poland.

As the months of my stay went by, my uncle gave me every little thing I asked for. At first I thought he was just kind, a family member I could establish a connection with, but it wasn't long before the attention he was giving me wasn't that of what an uncle gives his niece.

It started with conversations that should never have taken place, moving up to small touches, then he would ask me to show him how I looked in certain outfits he had bought for me. These all made me uncomfortable, but I didn't say a word. I needed to be here, and my aunt already had doubts about me.

Over time, things escalated to further levels of sexual harrassment and abuse, but I continued to let it happen. In my mind, I could not lose this place to stay; I could not get sent back home. Plus, at the time I told myself that my uncle wasn't actually *doing* anything to me. Everything came in the form of requests, flirty words, looks that shouldn't be happening, but I didn't feel like I was in any *danger*. I persuaded myself to believe this was okay behavior when it wasn't, because the consequences of calling attention to it seemed like they'd be worse for me.

Besides, Tim and I were writing love letters back and forth and I felt like our relationship was moving in the right direction again. We were making plans for our "happily ever after" and I didn't want anything getting in the way of that.

At the end of my stay in the States, I rushed back to Poland to see Tim. Everything from before my trip had been forgotten; our love was once again magical and perfect. Even the ugly moments of my vacation were gone from my mind, because all I thought of was him being happy, and thus me being happy with him.

It wasn't long until the fairytale dissipated. I shared the exciting news of my relationship's comeback with my best friend, and she showed me a letter from Tim that she received while I was gone that explained how he wanted to be with her. Then came the news of how Tim cheated on me while I was gone (with more than just one woman, and my "best friend" was one of the women). The feelings of betrayal ran deep. My heart was broken, and yet again, I had no one to rely on. I was alone.

The news about Tim shook me to my core; not only was I treated awfully by him, but the family I had in the States - the only people who could possibly help me escape my life in Poland - wanted to treat me as if I was anything but family.

Utterly devastated, I started to consider ways to end my painful struggle. I fought to sustain my relationship at the cost of my worth as a human being, and it was laughing back at me. Even with the new knowledge of Tim's behaviors while I was gone, I was still madly in love with him. The thought of leaving him left me feeling broken. I wiped up my tears, hoping I could somehow forget any of this ever happened. I wanted so badly to gain strength, to comprehend and accept the life I planned with Tim was a reality that would never be. His was the love I never even knew to dream about - love I didn't know existed - and here I was, ending it.

"I wanted to give you the world, lost little girl."

Very often, our first story of love is naive and blinded. When we are in the moment, our lives feel like a whirlwind; everything feels like a fairytale that we want to repeat forever. If the relationship ends, it feels like we'll never find something so amazing again. Therefore, we tend to hold onto it as long as we possibly can, refusing to let go, trying to feel the butterflies forever. Afterwards, we carry the memories of our first love into every new chapter of our story. Little do we know that there is so much more life waiting for us on the other side.

Chapter 12

New horizons

The unknown and feelings of uncertainty became my best friends in each new phase of life. Before I knew it, my ability to make a decision without asking anyone for permission struck. I was calling my uncle to rescue me, pretending like nothing had happened when I visited before. I knew exactly what to say so he would let me come back. His behaviors were going to affect me again, but I cared more about getting out. I was more scared of standing still than of what would happen once I left.

I was 16 years old. I told myself that I was not afraid of the unknown life I would have with my aunt and uncle; what I was escaping from was worth the price of just about anything. The move took me across the globe, from Poland to Indianapolis, Indiana. The United States, my new home.

It took time to get used to my aunt and uncle's life, there were new conversations, explanations, and for the first time, I had to ask permission to do anything. It wasn't easy for me to adjust; everything was so different compared to the life I left. On their end, my strong personality was definitely not something my aunt and uncle signed up for. I wasn't used to being checked on, and I let them know it. The reason I came was for freedom, and I realized in living with them that I actually had a lot of it in Poland.

Being back with my uncle was a challenge, as I spent mornings with him while my aunt was at work. Over time, I became pretty drained battling language directed toward me that was nowhere near appropriate. As a teenager, I didn't know how to tolerate it or what to do. Small touches started out as a form of care, but over time developed into more touches with less care. I couldn't gather my thoughts to figure out how to put a stop to what was happening. I felt like my world had opened up exponentially in leaving Poland, but I was trapped once again.

The mornings dragged on and I knew things would get worse before they could ever get better. I bought a recording device and devised a plan. One morning, I started using the recorder in my conversations with my uncle. I would talk to him like everything was fine, and the device would pick up all of his responses. I continued doing this for a few weeks, until one day he changed it up completely, throwing me onto the bed and forcing kisses onto my body. He held my hands down and attacked my face and neck with his mouth. I began to cry, begging him to let me go. He released me, but the damage was already done. I had every noise, every moment of my discomfort, recorded for the world to hear. Now, I just had to keep the tape safe and wait for the right time to share it with my aunt.

It took a lot of courage to look her in the eyes, tell her about what her husband was doing to me, and play the recordings I had made.

One afternoon when my uncle was gone and my aunt came home from work, I sat down with her and told her everything. Her first instinct was to not believe me, which was to be expected. I was the worst, the mess of the family.

Then I took out the tape and played all of the recordings. She was devastated. After 30 years of marriage, her entire life was being flipped upside down. However, even though she could hear everything my uncle was saying on tape, it didn't change the fact that to her, this was all my fault. She started firing questions at me, "What were you wearing?" and making comments about the bikinis I put on to sit out by the pool. She brought all of the guilt I felt for seeking help in the past bubble to the surface.

The decision to tell my aunt about my uncle's abuse was an extremely hard one to make. The two of us held onto the secret for as long as we could; I didn't even confide in my family back home for the longest time. Eventually, my aunt left her marriage and life took on a different kind of "normal."

The guilt that plagued me when I first conversed with my aunt faded away. What happened to me was not my fault. I never asked for my uncle to do what he did and it took immense courage to get out of that situation. I finally realized that my aunt's perception of me - the person she thought I was, the fact that she blamed me for her marriage falling apart - was not my responsibility.

My uncle "forgave" me faster than my aunt did, and got me to a place where I could forgive him. He was the reason my life had a new beginning, and despite his abuse, I was grateful to him for that.

I made peace with my choice to forgive my uncle by deciding not to look back on that time of my life. The two of us were able to truly bond, and some people might not believe it, but we created a beautiful friendship together. The two of us kept in contact for a long time after he and my aunt separated.

As the years went by, the love and care we had for one another grew in the purest way. My uncle called me one evening to tell me how much it meant in the story of his life for me to have forgiven him, how much it meant that I gave him another opportunity to do the right thing. He shared that when he died, he wanted his ashes to be thrown in Poland, over the biggest river in Warsaw.

Three days later, he was found dead in a motel room. He drank himself to death, and I was the last person he ever spoke to.

Forgiving my uncle and subsequently loving him was the best decision I ever made. It brings pain and tears to my eyes each time I talk about those last moments with him.

Today, he is gone, and my family knows the truth of how he treated me all those years ago. They don't agree with my decision to forgive him, and they don't understand how I could have chosen to create a meaningful relationship with him after what he did to me. Nonetheless, I continue to be grateful for who he was in my life.

As I share this story, I hope you will dive into your moments of pain, fear, and judgment of others. It isn't easy to forgive people in our lives when they do despicable things, and everyone's experience with trauma is different. For me, forgiveness was the answer; maybe it will help someone else.

"To forgive the ones who hurt us is the highest form of love and the most rewarding thing we can do, not only for them but for ourselves. Please, be willing to forgive, even when you're unable to forget the pain. Sometimes, trust can be rebuilt; peace can be replaced. Forgiveness will never change our past, but it will always change our future."

It can be so wonderful to stop going through life with shadows, always carrying the memories of pain. Letting go of darkness to instead let forgiveness bring in the light can be the best way to start living again.

I am living, breathing proof of this. If I chose not to forgive my uncle, I know that the pain I'd carry with me today would irrevocably weigh me down.

As much as we can, let's choose forgiveness.

Rest in Peace - In memory of my uncle.

Chapter 13

Awakening

"Forgive so you can be free of hurt." - Unknown

I entered yet another new phase of life rather quickly, this time, it was just me and my aunt. After a monumental change in her life - walking away from her multi-decades-long marriage - she was finally free. She was in love with her new life.

I made sure her days and nights were filled with unforgettable moments. She was able to feel young again, and our relationship became stronger with each passing minute. We were both happy and free, friends more than aunt-niece, and it was wonderful. All the worrying she did about me in the past began to dissipate.

As time went on, we got to know each other for who we really were, and my aunt began to understand that I held experiences which were completely different from those of a typical 17-year-old kid. She decided she could treat me like an adult, and my world opened up.

By this time, I was undocumented. My visa had expired, but I refused to return to my life in Poland. Why would I do that, when things were just starting to get good here? My plan was to never go back, and I called my parents to let them know this. My next step was trying to maneuver undocumented life without earning any wages.

Money became a struggle pretty quickly, as my uncle had been the main provider for my aunt (and me) for a long time. It wasn't an easy decision, but I knew I had to get a job - even though I spoke no English and had no legal documentation to work in the U.S. We searched and searched until I found a job as a cleaner.

Now, let me lay it out for you - I didn't know how to clean anything. Toilets? Carpets? How? I questioned my ability to do anything in that job, but I was determined to do anything I could to get to the point of supporting myself financially. After I became acquainted with my job responsibilities and began earning, it was time for some fun. (For that, you never have to ask me twice!)

My aunt and I started going out together - clubs, bars, on double dates, you name it. Looking back, I can understand how strange it sounds, but that was our way of life. We did everything together.

This lasted a short time, as eventually she grew tired of me always wanting to have fun. I was once again "out of control," and she got jealous. When I would go out without her - after all, I was a young woman who wanted to date around and party, not hang out with my aunt 24/7 - she got angry. To me, it was a sign that she was feeling lonely. She had divorced my uncle already, and when I was out having fun, she was left in an empty home.

My aunt didn't take well to me being gone all the time, but I didn't take well to her increasing demands for control. After all, I couldn't really handle it when I was 13, why would I now? Shortly, I was given an ultimatum. Either I conform to her rules, or I get out. At 17 years old, with no car, no money, no spoken English, no friends or family within thousands of miles, leaving was a scary thought. To make matters worse, she told me that if I chose to leave, she would report me to the authorities for being undocumented and I would be deported. Even though I felt like my only option was really *to* leave, I didn't have the slightest idea of where I'd go.

In the end, I did what my heart told me to do. I ran away. At first I didn't go far; the guy I was dating at the time lived in the same apartment complex as my aunt and I stayed with him in his 2-bedroom apartment down the street. Mind you, he had nine roommates besides me. He and his friends were Mexican, I was Polish, and none of us really spoke any English. It was definitely a challenge.

My aunt found out where I was staying eventually, and she continued her threat to deport me if I didn't come back to her. With her connections, she made it impossible for me to rent anything local; every office knew not to rent to me. I saw two options: call my parents and tell them everything, or leave again and tell no one. For better or for worse, I chose the latter.

No one had a clue as to where I was. I kept very little communication with anyone, as I was absolutely terrified to be caught and sent back to Poland. My parents did find out I was "missing" and they became so worried. My father grew anxious and angry, blaming his sister. "How could you let this happen?" Where is my daughter?" My aunt didn't have the answer, I had just disappeared.

I share this story not to villainize my aunt, but to continue talking about forgiveness. My time with her when I was young did not end in rainbows, but when I found myself in a better place, I reconnected with and forgave her. Years after this all took place, we spoke and saw each other again, and decided to remain in each other's lives. We each visited the other's home, we met each other's loved ones, and we developed the true aunt-niece relationship we should have had in the first place.

So that brings me here again: When faced with tough situations where people have hurt you, ask yourself not if you are *ready* to forgive, but if you are willing. If the answer is yes, work toward that. With each new day, the choice is in your hands, not in the hands of the one who caused you pain.

Chapter 14

Unknown destination

"Love is everything and can be everything, but one thing it can't be is uncertain." - Unknown

I said before that as a young girl I lost my feelings of fear. I learned how to not be scared of people or situations, because there was no room for fear in my decision-making. However, living in a strange country with no knowledge of the language, no support from family or friends, no way to get a legal job, no high school education, no driving abilities, no money, and no plan meant I was downright terrified. In my eyes, I was destined for failure.

Without knowing what the future held for me, I found myself a passenger in an older woman's car that I came across months ago searching for a place to rent and she happened to be the leasing agent that wasn't able to help me to rent an apartment I was looking for because of my circumstances.

Explaining my current situation with my aunt brought a soft spot in her heart and next thing you know We were on the highway headed toward a city called Miami. So far, my only known skill was convincing people to do what I wanted; it might have been the only skill I had. She was brave enough to pick me up when I asked her to, and I was brave enough to embark on another journey toward the unknown.

I was lonely and disappointed at how things had turned out, but I knew I had to find the strength to see this through. Otherwise, it was sure that I'd end up right back where I had been trying to escape for years. To me, this move truly marks the beginning of my "new life" across the globe.

The woman who drove me to Miami also decided to welcome me into her home when we got there. Her name was Tania, and she was kind and genuine just for the goodness of it. I knew it would only be for a few days, but it meant so much to me that I had somewhere to sleep after landing in a completely new reality.

Tania was only spending a couple of weeks in Miami while visiting her sons; her main home remained in Indianapolis. That meant I had two weeks to figure out my next move, or else be sent back to Poland (or to my aunt). I thought I was in desperate need of rescue.

Little did I know that a charming prince would take me away on his horse and tell me everything would be okay!

Well... sort of. Tania took me sightseeing, and the first few days in Miami were a magical vacation. I basically forgot why I landed there in the first place. One evening, she decided it was time for us to go dancing. We were going to have some fun and neglect all my struggles for just a bit.

Today I can truly say Tania was the light I needed and the guidance I searched for. She was and is the person I will always admire for her care and courage to help others.

And that brings me to know "If i never said out loudly, I had and always will be truly grateful for the compassion and care you had showed me when i desperately needed a helping hand and love you had given me throughout my darkest moments"

And... there he was. Mid-thirties, tall, handsome, Cuban. He laid his eyes on me, two weeks from 18, and I no longer had an idea of what life would look like in the morning.

I was in a dark place. It appears that I have plenty of experience with that! No matter how many times it felt like I had been thrust into the light, darkness always seemed to find a way to overtake things once again. Being so far from home I was tired, discouraged, and this man seemed like a way to distract me from that for a little while.

With the little English I did know by this point, we began chatting. Chatting turned to laughing, laughing turned to dancing. He was the first person I really interacted with since coming to Miami (besides Tania), and he was fun. Our night turned into breakfast the next morning, then late lunch, then dinner, and before I knew it, my time was up. The entire two weeks had gone by in a flash with his company.

Even in that short time, we encountered many differences in each other. We disagreed on a lot of things, we argued. I knew in my heart that he was not good for me, and I reached a point where giving up on him seemed to make the most sense. On the day I needed to leave I was still hoping for a miracle, but the hope was fading fast.

We both agreed that we were wrong for each other, and acknowledged that my time in Miami had come to a close. It was time for me to return to Indiana, or even Poland; I knew I needed to stop running away. In my head, I knew I'd have to go back to my aunt if I wanted to stay in the States.

To say his goodbyes, he drove us to an ice cream bar. He said he wanted a few minutes more of my time to discuss things - our differences and why we couldn't be together. It seemed weird to me, but I didn't know any better. Before I knew it, he was proposing with a diamond ring inside of the ice cream. I thought, "How creative," but I mostly felt like my head was spinning. This was unreal. I mean really, who the hell proposes that quickly, without truly knowing the other person or their intentions?

And who the hell says yes?

Two weeks later, I was saying "I do" to a stranger I barely knew.

Chapter 15

Marriage and Lagos

"Respect yourself enough to walk away from anything that no longer serves you, grows you, or makes you happy." - Robert Tew

As I was now a married woman, I decided I needed to build back the identity I lost along the way to this point. I had to get my life on some kind of track, or maybe just start a totally new life as a totally new person. This meant letting go of who I had been up to this point in time. I had to now try my best to put myself together while staying in my marriage, struggling with a silent drug addiction with no connections to obtain what I needed. I was still just 18 years old, but I needed to grow up. It was time for me to be an adult; I had to learn how to be a wife and a woman in society. My husband started teaching me all about these things - how to drive, cook, do laundry, and dress appropriately. He helped me with all of these "life skills" that I had never been shown before. In his eyes he was teaching me how to be the perfect housewife, which I didn't mind in the beginning. However, I knew that I had always been independent, and there was no stopping that fire inside me.

Having no paid work, I decided my housewife education was over. I "graduated" in my mind and wanted to move on, so I stopped in at the closest bar and asked, in my broken English, for a waitressing job. To my surprise, I got it.

On my first night working there, I saw that it was definitely a more "manly" environment. The whole place was filled with pool players, many of whom belonged to a professional league. I found it so interesting how peaceful the play was, and became eager to watch the game. I started coming to work early and leaving late so I could learn how to shoot.

The idea of the league intrigued me; I was still in my head at this point but was excited at the prospect of playing pool professionally. Luckily, there was a man who frequented the spot whom I had the privilege to meet. His name was Whitey (now may he rest in peace) and he had begun playing pool at 12 years old. He was, at the time I met him, nearly 80, blind in one eye, and used a walking stick to support himself, but he still played with the tenacity and accuracy of a youngster. He was one of the greatest, and he coached me as I learned the game, guiding me to eventually play in my own professional games. Over time, Whitey wasn't just my teacher, he became part of my chosen family. He taught me everything he knew, and I became good enough to be on his team in the league. We were in it together. This was something I was extremely proud of, to be a league member of a sport with so few women.

Late nights at work became late nights of playing in tournaments instead of working. I wanted to play, so I did. My husband was not only unhappy with my decision to work at the bar, but he was also unhappy with the idea of me playing pool with so many men around. However, he knew he had no choice in what I did, as stubborn as I was, so he did his part to support my journey in the best way he could.

The job, and playing pool, was good for me, as I started to develop friendships and meet people I truly enjoyed being around. The best part was that the feelings seemed mutual. I met my first girlfriend at that bar. Her name was "Lina, and she was a beautiful soon-to-be nurse who opened up her circle of friends to me. I mean, *everyone* knew and loved her. It was so nice; I finally had my first group of friends in Miami. I didn't feel alone anymore. Lina introduced me to lots of people, but one I came across in particular will forever be etched in my mind.

His name was Mr. Lagos, and I couldn't keep my eyes off of him. After countless years of not feeling that "spark" after Tim, I felt it for the second time in my life. It didn't take long before I knew I was in love with a man who was not my husband.

This frightened me, as I knew that what - who - I wanted was not my reality. I couldn't face the truth, and I couldn't afford to ruin things with my husband.

The feelings of love were mutual, and Mr. Lagos showed up to the bar every day just to talk to me. My job became something I looked forward to, as I overlooked the fact that I was a married woman who was constantly picturing her life with another man.

We talked for hours each time I worked, and though I had many opportunities to physically cheat on my husband, I didn't. I couldn't bring myself to give in, so I left Mr. Lagos to wait. And wait he did.

A year went by like this, and my feelings of love grew stronger each day. We had still had zero intimate interactions, but this was about to change. We started with just hugs, then kisses, and only from time to time. I couldn't bring myself to go further, but I felt like I had to be physically connected to him somehow.

One day, I couldn't wait any longer. My husband took a trip and I was left alone in the house, so I invited Mr. Lagos over. We were both ready for a magical night. We sipped some wine and talked about what our future together could look like. The passionate kisses began, but still, I found myself unable to go any further. I knew it wasn't right, but it didn't feel right either. I stopped him, and it was like he couldn't believe it. He didn't understand what I was doing, and he became angry. Soon, he left, and I felt both relief and extreme sadness.

I knew I made the "right" choice by not crossing *that* line, but that didn't stop the flame between us. He continued to pursue me, showing up at the bar every day at the time I came in and not leaving until my shift was complete. I was over the moon in love with him, more so than ever. His consistency over the years was a large part of what attracted me to him.

I imagined that sooner or later, I would indeed begin a new chapter with him. It was strange to me; usually I made decisions quickly and carelessly, but not this time. Deciding whether to leave my marriage took the longest time, and I could never understand why... until I found out I was pregnant. It was wholly unexpected and at the time, scary, but I now know the inability to make the choice was the biggest blessing in disguise. If I had been able to make up my mind and leave, my son would not exist today.

My husband at the time was in reality a perfect husband to any woman searching for perfection.

He was a provider, handsome, successful, he cooked, he cleaned, he didn't ask for much, maybe that was the problem?

I had most definitely not planned on having a baby, as I wasn't in a great position within my marriage. I tried to be so careful with birth control from the very beginning of my relationship with my husband. Upon finding out I was pregnant, I found out I was more than three months along and that I was having a boy. I searched for the happiness I saw radiating from other expecting mothers, but I couldn't find any inside myself at that time.

The fear, sadness, and pain that I was feeling was draining the soul from my body; I felt like there was no way out. I couldn't look back and didn't know how to look forward. Just like that, everything changed, and my entire life felt like it was moving backward instead of forward. I started to feel depressed, ruminating about how I was having a baby with a man whom I couldn't see living the rest of my life with.

Struggling with my feelings toward Lagos didn't make it any easier, but I knew I had to tell him about the pregnancy. I went into the bar to tell him the news. Of course, he was upset; he wished we had slept together on our "magical night" so that he could wonder if the baby was actually his. That fantasy couldn't even be entertained and we both knew it. We looked at each other with the pain of regret, wishing we had been together at least once. If the baby could have been his, we would have been celebrating. Instead, we grieved.

Being as far along as I was in my pregnancy meant that it was too late to terminate it even if I had wanted to. I thought that meant we had reached our definite end, but he believed differently. To him, there was still hope. He tried convincing me to leave my marriage, made me feel so wanted and loved in my moments of utter despair by saying he would take care of me and my son once he was born. Lagos hastily made all kinds of commitments to me in those moments, and I wanted so badly to believe him.

My head was absolutely spinning with everything he was saying, but somehow my mind was still not made up. After only a little bit of wondering why, it finally clicked. I understood my confusion and indecision. It was taking so long to choose Lagos because choosing him would put me right into my mother's shadow. She got pregnant with my sister by another man before she met my father. When my sister was just a few months old, my dad came in and took over, becoming a father to someone else's child before he even had kids of his own to think about.

Quickly, I had to remind myself why I left home in the first place. I never wanted to follow my mom's footsteps, I never wanted to repeat her stories when it came to love. Thus, I did the opposite of following my heart, choosing to let go of Lagos, our love, and the idea of our life together. Instead, I knew I had to return to my husband and bury the emotions I felt for the man I truly loved.

Chapter 16

Try harder

"Love is blind."

Being unable to work at the bar during my pregnancy was the perfect way for my husband to get me to stay home again. I wasn't going to accept that, so I asked him to pay for a course so I could get my GED. Pregnant and at the age of 20, I got my diploma. You probably know already that I couldn't stop there, so I signed myself up for a program through a local tech school to become a nail technician. I was so proud of myself, it was like I was getting a law degree – what a beginning!

Now that I had a skill, timing was everything. As I got further along in my pregnancy, I worked for my husband and his car business. I learned everything from how to clean cars to how to sell cars and do all the necessary paperwork. Over time I became his personal secretary. You'd think being busy would make me happy, but no. I was working full time with him and still in school to become a nail technician, so time was pretty tight.

Successfully, I brought a child - my son - into the world. The excitement I saw other women experiencing still wasn't there for me. My marriage wasn't going the way I'd hoped, neither was my growth as a person, woman, mother, sister, nor daughter. I had isolated myself once again, becoming depressed for several months after giving birth. More than four months of postpartum depression meant that for all that time in my son's life, I felt like the most miserable person on earth.

I knew I had to get myself out of that situation, so I began working again. This time, I had a skill to market - I was a nail technician and could work in a salon. The only place that was willing to hire me was a little Spanish place; barely anyone spoke English. A language I worked so hard to learn was now completely useless to me at this job! Without understanding a word of Spanish, work was challenging. I refused to stay in a position of not comprehending what people around me were saying, so I practiced my Spanish. I listened to it day in and day out, on TV, the radio, and in conversations with people in the area. English did not exist to me anymore, as far as I was concerned. Within a few months of that immersive lifestyle, I was speaking like I was the one from Cuba!

Being able to speak Spanish made it so much easier to communicate at my job. I made a hundred dollars a week, though I didn't really need money or to work as my husband's career was becoming more and more successful. Starting as a salesman, he opened his own dealership, which provided me with everything

I needed to continue doing nails and helping him to run the business.

At last, I was living in certainty and stability. I was working, raising my son, and being a good wife to my husband. Even then, it didn't feel like "enough" to sustain me. Therefore, I decided to begin a journey in bodybuilding. I learned as much as I could about the industry and became obsessed with getting my body into its best possible shape. I woke up at four in the morning to train, get my meals prepped, you name it. Hours and hours were spent in the gym, and they slowly began taking over me. As I created imbalance in my life and started tipping the scales, the stability I had established with my family started falling apart again. The fights we had grew more disrespectful each day, as I continued not only to train at 4 a.m., but to come back from work and drag my few-months-old baby with me to my evening session. Often, he laid in his stroller, just looking up at me while I did my thing in the gym. At only a few months old, he was spending most of his time in the gym with me... he probably spent more time in the gym than many grown adults. To me, those training sessions were my time to feel strong, but it seemed like I was the only one who understood how necessary they were to my wellbeing.

I kept trying to figure out how to change my life, to figure out why everything seemed to be going in the opposite direction than I'd planned. I knew I didn't want any more kids, so I decided to get an IUD to prevent future pregnancies.

I kept working, training, and living my life the best I could. A year later, I was in perfect shape, and most importantly, out of my depression. I had finally recovered! I was free from any of my previous harmful addictions, and fully at peace with the life I had created with my husband and son. I was in a good place, which, until that point, was a place I hadn't spent much time.

Eventually though, as we all know it to be true, life must strike again. I drove to a gas station one day in the early afternoon and out of nowhere, I ran into Lagos.

Did I want to cry, or jump for joy? I didn't know. I had worked so hard over the last couple of years to make peace with that phase of my life, and just like that, I felt like I was 18 again - back at square one.

This time, I didn't hesitate with my feelings toward Lagos, so we finally had our true magic together. It happened with the belief that it would lead to our true love, a happy ending for the romance we had to put on hold for so long. This time, I was certain everything happened for a reason and we were meant to be together. There were two problems with this thinking: one was, of course, that I was still married, the second was that Lagos was no longer single.

We talked and texted over the next couple of weeks, picking up right where we left off as if we never separated. Then, without warning, he disappeared. Gone again from my life. Devastated, I thought, "How can the same person break your heart twice?" Acknowledging that I did it to myself by becoming involved with him again, my peace - along with my recovery - was gone.

We often tell our loved ones not to go back to something that broke them once unless they want to be broken again. In our own lives, however, we continue to repeat our own pain for as long as it takes for us to finally learn the lesson. Eventually, we must decide how much hurt is enough.

I guess for me, I had not yet experienced enough pain with Lagos. Days of silence turned to weeks, then months, and he hadn't come back to look for me at all. Our story repeated itself once again, almost down to the T in the most mysterious way. The only exception was that this time when I received devastating news, Lagos wasn't there; I was alone.

I found out that I was three months pregnant. How? How is this possible? I can't have kids; the doctors said I'd have ten years of protection. It had been less than two since I gave birth the first time. Tears sprung to my eyes as I contemplated another adventure of uncertainty. I was more confused than ever.

This time, the man I loved could be the father of my baby, while my husband was the man by my side. I couldn't believe how the circumstances were turning out. I struggled to be a mother of one baby, let alone two. How would I do it?

With my family thousands of miles away, I was 23, in an abusive marriage, and about to have another baby that I couldn't see myself being well enough to take care of. A man I loved so much came back into my life, and I gave our romance another chance just for him to leave. I was disappointed and felt totally betrayed. Yet still, I couldn't find the strength to walk away from my husband. Our marriage no longer served either of us in a good way, but we held onto it despite the fact. If I couldn't leave that situation, how did I think I could ever turn the rest of my life around?

I became angry that I allowed someone else - Lagos - to take control of my life and my emotions. I was independent, this wasn't me. I needed to reassert my dominance in my own story.

Chapter 17

Wake-up Call

As the days passed and my reality settled in, I went to learn about all my options, specifically to see if there was one in which I could not go through with my pregnancy. I was given two choices, as I was once again way too far in my pregnancy to terminate it. I was told that if I continued on with the IUD inside my body, I'd be risking having a baby with health complications. On the other hand, if I chose to have the IUD removed, it would be 65% likely that I'd lose my baby during the procedure. As I write this now, only God knows how much I prayed not to have another baby. So, I chose to remove the IUD, willing to risk the pregnancy, knowing I was nowhere near equipped to raise a baby with significant health needs.

The procedure took 45 minutes, and afterward the doctor did an ultrasound to check on the baby. Soon, I got the news... "Congratulations! The baby didn't even move one millimeter, and you are having another baby boy!" I was frozen, speechless. Words can't even begin to describe the feelings I had in those moments.

I thought, "God, why has this happened to me?" I felt the worst pain I had ever felt in my life.

The next day, I woke up and enrolled myself in beauty school. I was going to become a skincare specialist. I went back to work full-time as a nail technician, did school part-time, and was four months pregnant with a one-year-old at home. Despite the challenges, I had to keep my faith. To this day I wonder where this sense of "faith" comes from in my life; I never had a mentor, guidance, or support through these tough times. However, I believed in myself enough to know that I could turn my life around.

As I continued my journey, learning to be a wife again as well as a mother to my son, I graduated from my tech program and had my second baby. At 24 years old, I was a mother to two healthy boys. Three months after my son's birth, I got a job as a dually-licensed beauty technician in one of the best hotels in Miami Lakes. Feeling like I was finally, truly taking charge of my life, I told myself that this opportunity would be my time to shine.

As for my life as a mother, I went to many doctors with the goal of figuring out how to stop another pregnancy from happening. Unfortunately, being only 24 meant I was too young for these types of procedures to take place legally in the U.S. Instead, I was given birth control injections, uncertain but praying they would be successful.

I was once again getting to a good place with myself. Continuing to live in my abusive relationship, I trained harder than ever before. I got into the best shape of my life; all I wanted to prove was that even though it felt like everything was falling apart on the inside, the outside could still look amazing. Every day, I woke up and showed up to be the best I could be, and it was paying off. I was becoming a stronger person, physically and mentally.

A year had gone by when something didn't feel right. I thought to myself, "This cannot be happening." Doctors confirmed it was indeed happening; I was two months pregnant.

As I shared the news with my husband, we were both devastated. We knew our marriage was going nowhere. He told me there was no way we could have a third baby, and he gave me $250.00 to get an abortion the next day. I woke up, took the kids to daycare, and went to the clinic alone, in tears, not knowing what to do.

As I think back on it today, I can remember being on the operation table, ready to go, telling myself, "You can do it. Just do it." Minutes later, the doctor couldn't keep my body still. They gave me all kinds of medication to calm me, but nothing worked. I couldn't control myself and neither could anyone else. After a short time, the doctor said she couldn't continue with the procedure. She sat me up, gave me a slip with a written notice valid for two weeks, and said, "When you are 100% sure to continue, come back and I will take care of you."

I got dressed feeling disappointed in myself, scared to go home and tell my husband. I tried to think of a reason why I couldn't go through with ending a pregnancy I didn't want in the first place. As I opened the door to go out to the car, a woman ran up to me, grabbed my hand, and said, "God bless you and this child!" I sat in my car, crying myself just about to death. That day, I talked to

God more than I ever had before. "Why now, when I finally have the option to decide for myself, what changed?"

I gathered my emotions and decided that the next day, I'd be back. I was not having this baby.

When I opened the front door at home, I saw my husband impatiently waiting for me to give him the news. I announced, "Yes, I did it. We are not having the baby," as I poured myself a shot of tequila. This marked the beginning of my drinking problem.

I spent the next few days drinking myself to unconsciousness at my neighbor's house, trying to get to the point where I woke up and everything was all over. Days became weeks of me not taking care of anything. I couldn't get up, I couldn't find strength, I wanted to end my life. One early morning, I went back home and can remember saying to my husband, "I didn't do it. I'm having this baby with you or without you, so get out."

I didn't really know what I was saying, why I was making this decision, or most importantly, how I saw myself raising and supporting three children on my own. I guess I was hoping for him to care, to show some form of love toward me, but it didn't change anything in his eyes.

"Okay then... have it!" He got his stuff and left. So there I was, staring at my two sons, trying to come up with a plan.

I continued drinking some more, all the while knowing I couldn't continue this big disaster. I woke up the next day and searched for ways to better take care of myself and my children. I decided to enroll myself in school once again, this time to become a massage therapist. I had seen my co-workers at the hotel make double the money I did as a beauty technician, so it seemed like it was an option that was worth a shot. Every school said the program would be around 15 months and cost around $12,000... that wouldn't work, so I kept looking. A few days later, I found financial aid that helped me take a loan and joined the massage therapy program, trying desperately to get things going before having my third baby.

I went part-time at work, took on school full-time, and did my best to raise my one- and three-year-old children. My husband returned home, and we decided to work on our marriage. Giving him news of my program only enraged him further. He said he was able to fully support us, and he didn't understand why I decided to embark on a career in *this* profession. He kept coming back to the fact that all I'd be doing is touching naked men, and he became unable to control his anger. When he saw me studying, he'd throw my books across the room.

Each day, he punished me for my choices, but they felt right in my soul. I kept fighting and never gave up. Anyway, I knew it was a matter of time before I found myself alone and raising three kids, so I needed to be prepared. I fought like hell and pushed myself to my most extreme limits. I finished my massage therapy program three days before giving birth to my third son. People said that what I did was nearly impossible, but I knew it had to be done. I surprised myself by pulling out strength I never knew I had - training every day in the gym, working, going to school, raising my kids, and preparing for another baby to join our family. Despite any challenges, I did what I set out to do.

Those around me disagreed with me doing so much; to them, I was about to burn out, thus not being able to fulfill any of my roles in the ways I should. To me, burnout was not an option.

"I can't burn out, I'm not a candle." - Grant Cardone

Chapter 18

Choices

"Perfect I am not, but who are people to judge when they don't know what goes on behind the scenes?" - Agnieszka Sycewicz

As the days settled down again, I had three months to take the state test required to become a licensed massage therapist. It took a lot more time to prepare than I expected. At the same time, I got ready to have a medical procedure in another country so that I would never have another child again. This time, the decision was certain; I had ended up becoming a mother to three boys by just 26 years old when I did everything I could to not be a mother at all... I had to focus on other aspects of my life so that I could build around my children now.

I flew with my husband and children across the ocean for my surgery. I also used this opportunity to see my mom, since I hadn't seen her since I initially left Poland all those years ago. For the first time, she was able to meet all three of her grandchildren together.

I went through with the procedure, and just like that, that chapter of my life was done. As I look back now, I see the bigger picture of the miracles that took place when I thought they were tragedies. I can truly say that I wouldn't be the person I am today without my kids. They saved me before I ever knew I needed to be saved.

Only God knew what he was doing when he blessed me with my three boys. Everything I have done since, despite feeling selfish at times, was for them. Today, my kids are grown men who deserve to know how I lived my life. I promised myself that I would never have my boys searching for clarity, no matter what ugly truth they encountered about me. I was just a little girl when I became a mom, searching for survival. I was given not one, not two, but three little human beings to look after during a time when I had trouble looking after myself. My boys can remember a lot of the struggle we shared, but today, we are all living with freedom from the darkness that once took over our lives.

Chapter 19

Return of Lagos

"If I had only known back then what I learned many years later, if I had only been able to see the end from the beginning." - Elder Dieter F. Uchtdorf

I had my three children, my husband was home, I no longer feared getting pregnant again, my career was in a good place, pretty much everything in life felt like it was going alright. The last thing I planned for was running into the love of my life yet again.

"What's happening?" I asked myself. "Why was this happening again?" "How is it that I have an entire life outside of my past with Lagos, yet he continues to show up?"

I had now seen him three times in seven years. I told myself it was a sign; it couldn't be that I loved someone for that long and it *wasn't* a sign that he kept showing up. Despite everything that happened between us, I believed in the sign again; it was easier to believe what I wanted to be true than to believe reality.

The two of us talked and reflected on everything that had happened in our lives. Before we knew it, we had started another chapter of our love story. It's funny to think back now and realize how much we're willing to risk when we're in love, without truly understanding the price we might pay. We're willing to overlook our current circumstances and the likelihood of things changing. We also forget the disappointment we have experienced in the past.

So just like that, we started texting, then talking on the phone for hours. We began to meet each other any chance we could. Our love became a fairytale once again; it was like I was back in a dream. I felt as if I could rule the world with Lagos in my life.

For the first time in a long time, I truly saw a beautiful life in front of me with someone I loved. He just had to tell me that he was ready. Realistically, what made me think he would be "ready" to be with me? I had three little kids. Reality didn't matter though, I basically believed that the fairytale was already coming true.

We had a plan and words can't describe how real it all felt to me. He said he was ready and we went forward with pursuing our love at last. Days passed and I searched for the strength to leave my marriage. It only had gotten harder over time; we had been married for eight years and had three children together. However, I knew I had to take this step. One early morning, I woke up, turned toward my husband, and said, "I'm done. I can't do this anymore."

He didn't understand what had happened. In his mind, we were going to be together forever. He thought having the children meant I would stay. After all, if I didn't leave when it was just me, how could I when we had the boys to think about? In his mind, being financially unstable with no family to support me meant I couldn't leave him. My husband thought this was just another one of my breakdowns, but it wasn't. My life with him was over.

I knew that after our conversation there would be no going back, and I never did.

As I share this story, I'm still trying to figure out why I chose an unknown life again over one of almost a decade of security, especially when I had new little humans to keep in mind. I understood the lives of myself and my kids were in my hands, but I was selfish. I made the decision to leave my husband based on emotions toward someone else, which was a huge mistake.

Throughout my marriage, I learned so many valuable skills. My husband taught me so much. Many women - not only immigrants but women around the world - have a dream of finding a rich husband. They want to be wined and dined, they want to go shopping whenever they want, they want to spend what they want, how they want. I found that life without even looking for it. I was given the opportunity to live an "easy life" where I was taken care of by my husband but instead, I kept making decisions for myself. I took on unnecessary hardships and always used the most challenging paths - somehow made just for me - to get what I wanted. Nothing he could have given me would make me settle down to be a housewife or live like a princess.

Many of my girlfriends today are searching for what I walked away from by leaving my husband.

Over the years, my ex-husband and I held the biggest resentments toward one another. It was hard to come to any peace, but finally, after 12 years of fighting post-divorce, we forgave one another. I searched for this moment for the longest of time to when we can look each other in the eyes and say sorry to one another and i made that happened even tho it wasn't an easy process facing each other we were finally able to say

I'm sorry, I forgive you. We shed a lot of tears over how our life was when we were together. Now, we are in a very good place. We remain friends and try to be the best parents we can be for our kids.

Despite the journey in my marriage he remains one of the most extraordinary human beings I had in my life who truly taught me so many valuable lessons in life I didn't see before. I was just not ready for what he had to offer me, and sharing this story isn't easy and it's definitely painful.

I remain forever grateful to have him as my first and only husband.

Chapter 20

Blinded by Love

I was feeling guilty about my decision, so I decided to leave everything behind. I only took my clothes, the children, and a crib for my youngest son. I had a broken car, lots of debts, and no secure income, but I didn't want to take anything my husband had worked his entire life for. I walked away empty-handed as far as material possessions goes, waiving all rights to alimony or the half of his money and business that was offered to me as his ex-wife. I truly believed that I would prove to him that I could be successful on my own. However, thinking this way was selfish once again; if I were thinking of providing the best life for my children, I would have done things differently.

The most painful part of leaving was listening to my husband, in tears, asking for another chance. He explained that he finally understood the care I had been seeking for eight years, and that he wanted us - me, him, the kids - to stay together. Unfortunately, my mind was made up, and it was too late. As I went through my divorce, my love life was actually heading in the direction I had been craving for a long time.

Once everything was said and done, I was in an empty apartment, sleeping on the floor with two kids and a newborn, who was only two months old and asleep in the crib I took with me. Things were happy, I thought.

A month of fairytale with Lagos turned to brutal reality very quickly, as one evening, the man I loved so deeply said, "I'm sorry, I can't do this." Just like that, in a matter of weeks, the love story I had created in my head for over 10 years ended in a blink of an eye.

That was a nightmare. I had broken down, and this time, I didn't see myself ever picking up the pieces.

I had finally hit rock bottom, and I didn't want to live anymore. I remember it as if it was yesterday. I had decided to end everything for myself, so I closed the kids in one of the rooms of the apartment. I asked for forgiveness in silence, asking God to watch over my sons, and took myself to the balcony with a bottle of wine.

"How did I get here?" I asked myself this question repeatedly as my face became streaked with tears. I didn't know another way out, and the pain felt too heavy to carry all on my own. The guilt and blame was taking over, and I could see the end to my existence.

I made the decision to call my "one and only," "la tati," my rock. The one who was always there for me during my worst times. The purpose of the call was to say goodbye, to say "thank you" for always being there, but that at 26, I had reached the very darkest place I'd ever known, and I could not carry the responsibilities of my life anymore.

As I made the call with my broken voice, he kept me on the phone for as long as he could. Without me realizing it, he was on his way - in the middle of the night - to save me from making what would have been the biggest mistake of my life. Now that I am out of that dark place, I truly don't know how hastily I had made the decision to end my life. I don't know now how I even thought of such a thing. All I know is that everything in life happens so quickly, and if we have even one person who truly cares, they will be there to take you out of your darkest moments. I know it because that's exactly what happened to me. Despite all the hard times I had been through before getting to this point, this was where I broke. I still consider it the darkest place I've ever been, to this day. Your plans for life will be derailed many times. Sometimes, you will feel like you are out of control and occasionally, you might not think you see a way out. I've learned that the most important thing is to build strong friendships, because as you are walking along your own path, one day, those friends may be all you could ever need to start again.

The words of wisdom and support I got that night have pushed me to open my eyes each day and press forward on my journey, even if I feel alone.

Even though at that time, I still probably could've gone back to the life I had with my husband, full of stability and security, I chose the hard road once again. I chose to fight, in the hopes of one day finding my true peace.

Chapter 21

Rebuilding from Scratch

"When we analyze the choices that brought moments of disappointment, betrayal, and pain into our lives, we realize that a major step toward peace within ourselves is to forgive and be forgiven."

As my recovery began, I started to rebuild my identity as a single mom, starting from the bottom.

Never knowing what "tomorrow" held for me, I started to think that maybe I had to let go of the life that I planned to accept the life that had been given to me. That was a notion I had always disagreed with before, but time and time again it showed itself to be at least partly true.

When the unexpected entered my life, I began to let go of the fantasy I had created over the years. I decided to have a little fun, accepting the fact that I wouldn't have a serious love life anytime soon. After all, it's not often that you meet someone, tell them you have a six-month-old baby, an almost-two-year-old, and a four-year-old, ask them out, and receive an enthusiastic yes. I learned that things just happen in life, and it's easier to go with the flow than to try controlling everything.

A man approached me one evening in the club. It was my first night out as a single woman. He said "Hi, what's your name?" I looked at him and responded, "You don't even want to go there?" The next thing that came from him was, "Why not?"

I believed that this was the moment I was about to experience my first rejection in my new phase of life. I began my spiel: "I just had a baby. And not only that, I have two others; one is two and the other one is four."

To my - and to my single, non-mom friends' - surprise, he said what I said and came back with, "...and?"

There it was, the beginning of a new chapter in my life. I asked myself, "How did this happen so quickly?" As I tend to do, I jumped. One night turned to dating; three months later, he was moving in with me and my kids. My ex-husband, my ex-love, my friends, everyone was quite surprised.

I had been blinded by love yet again, but this time I was blinded by the love and support he gave to my children. Life was natural with him, he loved the kids magically and the support he provided was one-of-a-kind. He made me feel as if I was the only woman on the planet. For someone who had learned what abuse could look like pretty early on in life, I couldn't see anything indicating what was to come.

My friends reminded me all the time to be careful, to watch over myself. I lost a lot of friends during this time; they wanted me to choose between my relationship and my friendship - so I did. Clearly, they saw the red flags that I missed. I truly thought no one would ever love me and my children the way he did. This belief led me to safety, but unknowingly also to danger. I was repeating an old story again without even seeing it.

To me, I was moving on. I was forgetting Lagos, I was recovering my mental health, I was healing. One night, Lagos showed up at my door like the true ghost from my past that he was. He had many convincing words as to why I should give him another chance, why he shouldn't have ever let me go, but I was fed up. These were the words I had been waiting to hear leave his mouth for years, but now it was too late. I had moved on. Being in my new relationship made me realize that waiting ten years for Lagos was the biggest fantasy that would never become reality. The future I saw with him for so long had dissipated.

It had only been a month since Lagos left by the time he showed up at my door, but I was already taken by someone who showed up in my life at the absolute worst of times. I continued to move in the direction I was already headed, rather than go backwards. I knew where saying "yes" to Lagos would take me, and I thought it would be less painful in the end to propel myself further into the unknown.

Right then and there, I took a chance on myself. Instead of jumping back into old patterns, I decided to change the narrative. I learned over time that it was better to live paying the price for my choices when I actually took control and decided, as compared to how it was to live paying the price of regret for standing still. It was a moment of clarity that I could be proud of, and I try to carry it with me to this day.

Heartbroken and leaving two broken hearts behind, I did begin to see an obsession developing in my new relationship. Our passion for each other became stronger and stronger each day, the fights we had became so sick and our love so fierce that neither of us knew how to walk away. It's as if we were drugs to one another. We knew we were harming each other and ourselves, but we were addicted. We kept finding each other over and over again, knowing the recipe was dangerous.

As the kids started to grow up, money became tight. I worked as a nail technician and esthetician and he worked nights as a security guard, but our incomes were not enough to pay the bills. My dream of becoming a licensed massage therapist was slipping away with each passing day. Therefore, I had to make a choice: study for the exam, or get another job.

I picked up a night job as a cocktail waitress at a place next door to my boyfriend's work... wow, what a power couple, right? This meant working mornings at the spa, taking care of the kids in the evenings, and getting a babysitter every night so I could work another shift with no sleep. It wasn't what I'd call easy, but I told myself repeatedly that this was my reality. I told myself that I was making a life with the only man who would choose me as I was, and that had to be enough.

Paying the bills got easier with the additional job, but our relationship only got worse. The club scene was growing, our obsession with each other was becoming more trapping. There was jealousy and insecurities on both of our parts. The verbal abuse became more hurtful. Red flags showed more clearly. I began to feel unsafe, but stayed. I felt so attached to him, like the bond I had with him was too strong to break. People around me started calling him "Jesus Christ," because the power he had over me was unmatched.

Years passed like this, and I grew so tired. I was in another situation that I didn't know how to get out of. I wanted to leave, but I also didn't. I had gotten to a point where almost everyone I had in my life was gone. They all said it was a matter of time before something bad happened, but I was so far in denial - even when they proved to be right - that I chose to lose them rather than lose him.

One random early morning, I received a text message from Lagos. So much time had passed since he stood at my doorstep, but he still couldn't let things go. My boyfriend knew about my past, he knew how strong my feelings would always be for Lagos, he knew way too much about me. When I reached for my phone and saw the message, he saw it over my shoulder and absolutely lost it. He attacked me, choking me to the point where I thought I was going to die. All I can remember now is looking up toward the ceiling with tears streaming down my face and no air in my lungs, only seeing stars. Words cannot even explain how desperately I tried to get my son's attention, as he was in another room, for help.

At that moment, life ended for me. I felt paralyzed, mentally, emotionally, and physically. Afterward, I couldn't speak, eat, or sleep. I stayed barely conscious from the shock for three days, watching my boyfriend take care of my kids while I couldn't do a thing for them. My brain felt frozen, and my body felt completely drained of strength.

He behaved as expected, getting on his knees, crying, trying to bring me back to myself. "Please say something, I'm so sorry..." "Please eat." He didn't understand that nothing he said could ever take back the fact that he almost killed me with my children in the next room.

I don't know what did it, but on the fourth day I got up in slow motion. I remained calm, and I told him it was time for him to pack his stuff and leave.

It finally became so clear that just because people give us value doesn't give them permission to abuse us in any way. That was a true awakening for me, to take a step back and decide I would never repeat that aspect of my past again. I would never again tolerate anyone in my life taking away the peace I fought for.

I had to remind myself why I was here, why I had come this far, and where I wanted to go. I realized that being truly, deeply loved by someone else should give me strength and power, rather than paralysis, fear, or obsession. At the same time, I realized that truly, deeply loving someone else - like the way I love my kids - gives me courage.

As I began looking toward the future, I knew there was one thing that would help me on my journey to ultimate change: forgiveness. This included forgiveness for those who had caused me pain, sure, and I talked about similar notions before. The list wasn't long, but it was hard to forgive the people on it. Along with that, this time, I counted myself as someone to forgive. I made choices that brought me pain and were not the best for my sons, but I wanted to be better. The only way to start being better was to assure myself that I had love, forgiveness, and kindness to offer the woman who looked me in the eyes when I stared into the mirror.

Chapter 22

Times of Survival

"The road to recovery is never without obstacles, challenges, or triggers, but never forget your life is worth the fight against substance abuse." - Unknown

Forgiveness was just one piece of the puzzle, and the other pieces for me were still being sorted out. I moved on to another chapter in my life's story carrying a lot of pain and discouragement. Though in some aspects, I knew how to get better, in others, I clung to old, destructive habits.

The situations I put myself in where there has been no respect for my life or emotions have been the hardest ones to endure. In trying to forget the past and escape the pain of the present, I was becoming more lost than before - even though I wanted to see the light.

Working two jobs didn't bring in enough money for me to survive and take care of my children, so I found myself working extra shifts in other places I'm not proud of. Leading up to this point, I hadn't touched drugs in nine years, and it wouldn't have even crossed my mind as an option during that time. However, once I was struggling to care for my family all on my own, I made my way back to using drugs and alcohol as a way to lose all feeling.

In the depth of my addiction, days became nights and nights became days without me truly realizing time was passing at all. I got close with a colleague at work who I soon considered my friend, and the dark path she was on made my own that much easier to follow.

Friendships came and went, relationships were transient and served only as temporary relief for my pain. I couldn't see anything but darkness; there didn't appear to be anything to guide me in the right direction. I continued meeting people I didn't really care to meet and keeping people around who didn't deserve it. The other phases of my life contained crises because something (or someone) that didn't serve me was present; this time, my crisis came from a sense of emptiness.

Chapter 23

Trial of Faith

"To win, you have to risk loss." - Jean-Claude Killy

Over time, the reasoning behind our life's circumstances becomes clear. Events happen in our lives and we think, "Why me?" "Why now?" "How did this happen?" However, everything happens to teach us something important about how we interact with the world, whether we know it at the time or not.

Driving back from work in the middle of the night, I heard the sound of sirens behind me. I pulled over and was subsequently arrested for driving under the influence. I resisted showing proof of sobriety at the time of my arrest. Three police patrols took me to the station, where I spent the night in jail. I was offered a plea deal - pleading guilty to a DUI and completing one year of community service - and I refused. I'm not sure exactly what I was thinking by going to trial; if I lost, I faced up to a year in prison.

The process of a trial took over two years with my public defender. Even though I knew I committed the crime, I felt this sort of power within me. Everyone around me thought I was crazy. They told me how stupid it was not to take the deal and reminded me that I had too much to lose (i.e., my children) by risking prison time, but I didn't want to give up. I wanted to fight, and I wanted to win.

Amidst this crisis, I met a few different people who led me to a referral for a criminal lawyer. They took my case on the day of the trial. As I prepared to begin this battle in the courtroom, I was signing empty checks to give to my friends in case I didn't come out. I was hoping to leave some money for my kids while I was in prison and arranging for them to be taken to their dad's. My head was spinning with my reality, wondering what the next hours would bring.

As I saw the three police officers from the night of my arrest walking into the courtroom, I became overwhelmed. I needed a minute to think, so I went into the courthouse bathroom. I started crying, wondering why I was here. "Why am I doing this?" "Stop." "Take the plea deal and move on with your life!"

I began to pray so hard, making tons of promises to God about how I was going to shift my life around and make enormous changes. I prayed for guidance in the right direction so that I could better myself.

I knew I didn't have to go forward with a trial, I had a relatively "easy" way out. But there was something inside me that wouldn't allow me to let go and take the plea. It almost felt like I wanted to feel the rush of winning, but my brain wasn't considering the consequences that could come with losing... in my life *or* the life of my kids.

So, there I was, taking the stand, swearing on my life in front of the jury. I was cross-examined by the prosecutor. As I answered the lawyer's first question, I saw one of the witnesses and a police officer leave the courtroom. Then, a second witness got up and left. Then a third. I had no idea what was happening. The judge called my lawyer to the bench and said something to him quietly, before addressing me and the whole room.

"Can the defendant please stand for the final verdict?"

"Case dismissed..." I heard. "Wait, what?" Thoughts raced through my mind. What just happened? How did this happen?

I still don't totally understand what happened at my trial or how I got the outcome I did. All I know is that hearing the judge that day brought out the strongest version of me I have ever known. This time, I was determined, motivated, and dangerous.

I walked out of the courthouse that day with the highest tolerance for pain I had ever experienced, as well as the most gratitude possible for my life.

Chapter 24

Hope for Help

"When you reach the end of your rope, tie a knot in it and hang on." - Franklin D. Roosevelt

One sunny afternoon, I decided to take the boys to a park they loved, which was a little farther from where we lived at the time. When we got there, the kids practically jumped out of the car to play. Walking toward the park to watch over them, I saw a woman sleeping on a nearby bench who resembled my first friend in Miami, Lina - the girl who had had a whole nursing future in front of her.

As I got closer to the bench, I realized it was her. I gently touched her to wake her, astonished that I was meeting her again in this way. "Lina, what happened?"

As devastated as she was, she replied, "Oh my goodness, it's so good to see you. It's been so many years!" We started chatting and she shared her story of battling with drug addiction and losing her home and son. Her family and friends had long since given up on helping her, so she was homeless and all alone. After a few hours of talking, she confessed that she also had an affair with Lagos. "You mean to tell me you had sex with Lagos, the man we all knew was the love of my life?"

While apologizing and asking for forgiveness, she could barely make eye contact with me. Finding out about the affair years after the fact and seeing her in this state, it would have been all too easy to walk away from her. Except I couldn't. I pulled her close and hugged her, got her in my car and took her home with me and the boys. I bathed her, gave her some clean clothes, and took care of her. We made it work, even with as little as I had. The next day, I called out of work so I could set my sights on trying to help her find a more permanent solution. I looked into every possible rehab center, standing in long lines at each one, praying I would find someone who could help me help her. In the end I took weeks off of work, waking up at 4 a.m. each morning, bringing her along to every new place I found, all while another one of my friends watched the kids and made sure they got to school on time.

The long days and longer lines left us with no hope day after day. We were constantly being rejected, as there was no space anywhere to place her. Each day we returned home with no solution, disappointed and with diminishing hope. As I was trying to help my friend get the support she needed, I was still trying to make ends meet for my kids. But I couldn't let her walk away.

It was a struggle to keep her in my house, as those around me were against me having a drug addict living in the same place as my kids, but I didn't listen. I reached out to everyone I knew but still nothing. Nobody was willing to get involved with her, especially once they knew she had failed each time she attempted to go to rehab in the past. After almost a month of having her in my home, I took her to church - a place that had been a source for my motivation and strength over the years. When we got to the church, I reached out to the pastor and shared Lina's story, despite her refusing to come up with me. The next thing I knew, the pastor appointed us to a rehab center that agreed to take her. We were overjoyed. We gathered in a circle with strangers in that church, prayed, and cried.

I drove Lina to the center the next day. I was so proud of her and visited every weekend, making sure she stayed on track with her recovery. I brought her money, candies, cigarettes, anything that could help her get through the miserable path she was on.

The day I dropped Lina off at the center brought one of those moments where I wished someone would care for me in the same way, but it was also the day I began to see myself not as a victim, but a warrior. I looked back on my days of addiction, and the struggles I faced when I didn't have a single helping hand. I realized I had something special in me; I had some kind of drive to get up on my own, each and every time I fell.

My friend Lina finally recovered. It was a miracle, and I was honored to continue being the support she needed. After she left the rehab center, we found her a place to stay in a small apartment on the beach and got her a job with a friend of mine who owned a hotel. She was truly doing great. Some time later, her parents reached out to me. They never really liked me, presuming I was a bad influence because of my appearance, but when they found out what I did for their daughter, they asked to come visit me.

We met and her parents gave me money in an envelope, saying they couldn't believe I was able to help Lina accomplish recovery, especially when the two of us had drifted so far away from one another. They asked, "How did you do it?" insisting they had tried everything to no avail.

I simply replied, "It takes faith when you see the impossible," and it was true. In situations where it seems like there is no solution, we need to hold onto our faith. Nothing more, nothing less. And that, the ability to cling to my faith when everything else was crumbling, was my gift.

Chapter 25

Not All Flowers Bloom in the Light

"Our human compassion binds us the one to the other - not in pity or patronizingly, but as human beings who have learnt how to turn our common suffering into hope for the future." - Nelson Mandela

While Lina's life was looking up, mine was still in a dark place. It got to the point where I had to make a pretty tough decision, and one I had been avoiding. I was still working two jobs but couldn't afford the things we needed - food, diapers, daycare, and rent. I didn't know what else to do, so I joined the Special Supplemental Nutrition Program for Women, Infants, and Children (WIC) to get food for our family.

Along with that, I needed to come up with a faster and easier way of making money so that we could start to climb out of the hole we were in. I decided to get a job in a strip club. I started just as a waitress, but after a few shifts of seeing how much attention and money the women could make, I made the transition to the stage.

While I didn't take pride in having this job, as I have said before, everything happens for a reason.

For the first time, I was able to relate to the struggles of other women in that position. I was able to remove judgment I may have passed toward them during previous times in my life and adopt more compassion for the ladies in the industry. I realized I wasn't better than them; we were all fighting life in different ways.

In this position, I was able to learn from other women about different cultures, languages, and beliefs. I didn't really know anyone in Miami who came from Poland, and I associated more with being American than Polish by that point, anyhow. One evening, I came across a group of girls from Poland, which was quite unexpected. It was priceless, being able to experience people from home. It's funny to look back now and remember how girls who became such a big part of my life were, at one point, just strangers.

I felt like I had finally found the circle of women to which I belonged: Lola, Chichi, Asyiaa, and Julie. These girls were young, crazy, and full of energy, and I had to remember that I was the oldest one... who also had three kids. The girls lived in a different city. They planned parties and vacations; everything was just about enjoying life.

It was like I was a teenager again when I was with them, always surrounded by beautiful, single, young women. I knew they lived completely different lives than me, but I looked forward to hanging out with them anyway. As they had only recently immigrated from Poland, their vision was to make money and meet as many rich boyfriends as they could. Many of them still didn't have proper documentation to legally remain in the country.

After only a few days of knowing these girls, I went on my first vacation without children. I packed myself up and ventured to Las Vegas with them and had the time of my life. Being away from reality was nice for a bit, but it was all temporary - after the trip ended, I returned to life with the boys.

Throughout our time together, there was one girl in the group in particular with whom I clicked. Our bond gave me such a weird and indescribable feeling that I didn't remember feeling before.

Have you ever met someone who just seems to be a reflection of you? That's how I felt about beautiful 20-year-old Chichi. We liked the same things - same clothes, the same guys, same music, same type of people, everything. Out of everyone in our group, the two of us bonded on a whole other level. It was like we had been twin sisters in a past life. When the other girls stayed in a different city after our little vacation, Chichi found herself on a plane, headed back to Miami with me.

Chapter 26

Strangers Can Become Best Friends Just as Easily as Best Friends Can Become Strangers

Chichi had no place to live, no family, and no friends in Miami, so I offered for her to stay with me. I didn't see a problem with her living in my home for a while; after all, despite having only known her for a few days, it felt like we had been a part of each other's lives for years.

With her being only 20 years old, it kind of felt like I was adopting a fourth child. I wasn't really worried about how we would manage, but I did set expectations so she would know that living with me and my boys wouldn't be the same as living with a bunch of her single friends.

I didn't know much about Chichi at all, but I knew we got along great and that I wanted to help her. On her first day with us, I woke up realizing I took on quite a responsibility in letting her stay. She didn't have legal documentation and couldn't get a driver's license or job, so I wanted to help her get started on the process. While this was happening, I was still trying to keep myself and my kids afloat. I was driving a broken car and struggling to afford food. People didn't understand why I took Chichi in when I had so much going on, but I didn't see her as a burden. I was grateful to have met a wonderful friend.

With Chichi in my home, we got to know each other well. We went out together almost every day, and this time turned quickly into one of the craziest times of my life. But we could also be serious; I guided her toward getting the necessary documentation to stay in the States, we arranged for her to live with me more permanently, we signed her up for school so she could get a student visa, and I became her sponsor, which meant I agreed to take responsibility for any problems she encountered while in the country.

We started to create a life together; some people thought we behaved almost like a couple. As days and then months passed, our lives truly became like a marriage, as weird as that is to say - I worked a full-time job during the day and at the strip club at night while she helped me with the kids and the house. We were partners in crime 24/7.

We took a look at how we were living and decided my income was not enough to take care of the five of us. Things had to change, so Chichi started back up at the strip club, working nights with me. There I was again, working day and night, hiring a babysitter to watch my kids. I knew from previous experience that working night shifts was going to make things worse, but I felt a little more hopeful this time because I wasn't alone in it.

Working nights soon became party nights, and Chichi and I started to develop this strange, seemingly unconscious competition between one another. Maybe it was in my head at first; it was hard to be rejected by men because I had kids while Chichi got to choose whatever man she wanted. I valued her as a friend more than I envied her as "competition," but over time it became too much to handle - my behavior became too much to handle. I became angry that men I wanted to date wanted her, and vice versa for her. In the beginning, our lives together were fun, but after numerous situations where men were the central dilemma, resentment started to grow. Then, not communicating clearly and effectively about it made things worse.

All in all, this situation with my best friend taught me that whatever feelings you are experiencing in the moment deserve to see the light. They must be spoken and clarified to be understood, and if you value the person whose behaviors are throwing off your emotions, communicating openly will limit resentment and negativity.

Chapter 27

El doctor

"Angels aren't in Heaven, they are on earth. But not everyone is able to see them."

Fast-forward a bit and Chichi met an older man who fell in love with her. He was a very successful, powerful man who was in a great position to help her turn her life around. We called him, "El Doctor," and he assured us that we no longer needed to work nights.

As their relationship was blossoming, he also became friends with me and my friends. He wined and dined with us wherever we wanted. We traveled, going places we could only dream of just a short time before.

We got everything we wanted from him... at the price of him being with her. El Doctor was a way for Chichi to escape her struggles, but with time, I saw him as a way out of mine too. A month after they began dating, he came over, sat down at my dining table, and said, "Agni, tell me your struggles and I will make them disappear." I didn't quite understand what he meant by this; he was a semi-strange man dating my friend... what could I possibly expect him to do for me?

After talking for a while, I saw him reach for his checkbook. He asked "What do I owe to whom?" and he meant all of it. All of the debt I had incurred since getting divorced was about to be signed away. I was speechless... and so was Chichi.

Just like that, this man that neither of us knew extremely well randomly decided to pay off my debts - like I said, I mean everything. He paid debts from my marriage, school, credit cards, rent, and my kid's tuition. Everything I ever owed and more, and that was only the beginning.

One morning, we received a phone call from El Doctor saying, "Agni, it's time you stop driving your old broken car. I want you to go and look for a car you like." Again, I was left without words. "It couldn't be... how could this be?"

I wondered what he would do when the woman he was actually dating was without a car... he never tried anything with me but was so generous. I took him up on his offer and went shopping for a car. I didn't even know what I was looking for, so I sent him options of cars that were in the range of $10,000-$15,000. To me, anything like that was an absolute dream. He didn't take those options very well. "You deserve a better car, find yourself something better," he said. As a joke, I showed him a car worth $80,000. He got a salesman on the phone, wired the money, and put the car in my name. I thought this was seriously only something you'd ever see in a movie.

I drove away in a brand-new BMW M3. I didn't know whether to be happy for myself or confused and sad for Chichi; she was without a car and still living in my house. She looked happy for me, but I know it wasn't happiness she was experiencing at that time, it was envy.

When he returned from a trip back to his country, he furnished our home to our liking. He brought my kids to the toy store and gave them each a cart, telling them to grab whatever they wanted. I watched my children fill their carts with toys and games I couldn't even begin to imagine being able to afford. Life felt like a dream. EL Doctor turned my life around from the second I met him, and it never cost me anything to get what he so kindly gave me. Maybe it was the kindness that I offered him; the love and appreciation I have for him will always remain. If one day I could repay him for the joy he brought into my life and into the lives of my children, I would do it with every breath I had left. Something meeting him taught me was that if you stayed true to who you were, you could always expect the unexpected.

My work in the strip club only lasted a few months. From my experiences there, I learned that you can never know who you'll meet, how, when, where, or why, so it is important to always keep yourself humble.

El Doctor was the first person in my life who gave me something without asking (or demanding) something in return. He was a blessing for me and my boys; so much so that I neglected to pay attention to how Chichi felt about him or what it was like to walk in her shoes. It wasn't fair for him to give me all he did while she looked on from the side. I know in my heart that he was the source of a lot of the resentment that eventually grew in our friendship.

After realizing Chichi's suffering and the fact that she had stayed in a relationship she didn't want, I felt terribly guilty. From that, I took away the idea that paying a price to be with someone because you think *they* will pay the price is one sure way to be disappointed. I wanted so badly to help Chichi turn this around somehow, so I found a way to obtain her legal status so she could become a U.S. citizen. Then, the man who liked her so much started slowly drifting away before eventually, he disappeared forever. The fairytale was real, but it was short. We were back to the lives we lived before we ever knew El Doctor.

After he left, it didn't take long for us to go broke again. Instead of batting our insecurities united, we blamed each other. We got a notice that the lease would not be renewed for our apartment, and trying to rent another place with three children proved to be a challenge. Landlords kept saying no, pointing to noise as the reason they didn't want a family moving into their complex. On top of that, I didn't have good credit or money saved to move, and I was not willing to go back to working nights at the club. I had already had to sell my car - for less than half of what it was worth - to try and survive. All of our things went into storage and we rented a studio for a month while we sorted things out.

While this was happening, I got a phone call from Poland that my dad wasn't doing well. He had been diagnosed with bone cancer and his condition was only getting worse.

At this point, I hadn't seen my dad in nearly eight years. The first time I saw him after leaving Poland was when I had been gone for over a decade. While we weren't terribly close, the idea of him being alive and not meeting my youngest son was a thought I couldn't live with. Not to mention my other sons didn't even remember him; he had last seen my oldest when he was two and my middle son when he was six months old.

For the first time since my divorce, I called my ex-husband in tears, begging him to lend me the money to buy plane tickets to see my dad. He agreed, and I left Chichi in the studio, where the rent was about to expire, and headed to Poland.

Chichi had to move out before I would be returning, so I reached out to Lina and asked her to help. Amazingly, she was able to provide a temporary place for Chichi to stay until I got back. It's incredible how life turns around on you, always so unexpectedly. There were periods of such goodness in life, but they never seemed to last long enough. They had never been sustainable. During this time, we made the only choices we could.

I spent nearly one month in Poland, next to my dad who underwent a 17-hour surgery to replace his affected facial bones with bones from his hip, as the cancer took over his body. He was barely talking, eating, or moving by the time I had to return to Miami. I had no idea where I was going to live or how I'd afford anything, as I spent the last of my money while visiting my dad. Thus, I had to say goodbye to him and make my way back to figure everything out.

The day I returned, I found an apartment that was available for move-in that evening. The only problem was this: I did not have enough money for the deposit. Chichi and I desperately tried to gather the money; we sat in front of the grocery store counting every cent we had and calling all our friends to borrow as little as $100.00. For the entire day we did this, even getting a few dollars from strangers, until we had enough to put down the deposit. We moved in, and I found myself once again sleeping in an empty apartment... this time with my kids *and* a 20-year old whom I felt wholly responsible for.

Three days later, I received a phone call that my dad had passed away. It felt as if he had been waiting on me all those years. At that moment, I was struggling with money, yes. But I realized that the money would come back. It always did. However, the decisions you make, or don't make, are what stay with you forever. I was able to see my dad before he passed after not seeing him for almost a decade, all three of my children were able to meet him, and those things meant so much to me.

Living with regret is the biggest pain in life that we cannot change!

And so, life continued with another new beginning.

Rest in peace forever, Dad.

My friendship with Chichi had been going strong, but differences started showing up in our lives that changed our relationship dynamic. I started dating and finally, almost five years after she first started staying with me, she moved out of my house to be with her boyfriend. During that time, our friendship began to waver. We became so busy making our own lives that we forgot about our foundation. Mainly, Chichi was on a new path with new friends, and she wanted me to be separate from all of it. That was a painful feeling of betrayal; after all, she was my best friend. She was a part of so many memories and stories from the years since we met, but it was like I wasn't a part of anything for her unless I made it so.

Chichi's boyfriend didn't like me at all, despite barely knowing me. I took the fall for her on many occasions, getting blamed for late, crazy nights and her disappearances. I did it because I didn't want her to get in trouble, but even that didn't show her how much I cared about our friendship. Our time spent together was extremely limited and as much as she loved feeling independent, I think what she loved more was feeling independent from me.

I overlooked this at the time, but I now realize I was looking for the same thing in my friendship with Chichi as I had looked for in all my past relationships - to be important, to feel like someone truly cared to include and love me. However, friendships, like romantic relationships, don't always last. People grow apart, and that's what was happening.

Chichi started keeping secrets and continued going her own way. She reached back out after three years had passed, when we had almost completely drifted apart. She confessed to me that she had been living in misery and was trying to leave an abusive relationship. Chichi had hurt me a lot, but my heart was still weak when I knew she was hurting. I was no longer single and was living with my significant other, but I took her back into my home without a second thought. At the end of the day, she knew I had her back like no one else.

Being in the same place again strengthened our friendship like never before. She became a part of everything I did; I'd go so far as to say she became like a third addition to my relationship. The three of us ate together, took trips together, and spent tons of time together. Even on Valentine's Day, I felt guilty leaving her alone. Her feelings were more important to me than my boyfriend's or my own.

After spending some time helping her to heal from her previous relationship, Chichi found a new partner - someone kind, caring, and secure. He was someone she could rely on, a truly amazing guy. Then, all four of us were finally happy.

Chapter 28

Real estate

"To every door that closed on me: I'm coming back to buy the building." - Laura Clegg

Finding out years later that Chichi's dad was financially secure was a big surprise. There I was, without anything at all yet giving her everything I could, while her own family was well-off and never willing to lend a hand.

Randomly, he decided to give her some money to invest, and she came to me - knowing the connections I had - so we could go in together and seek an equal split on the profit. We chose to go into real estate.

We created a company, and months later bought our first investment property. It was a success. We pushed through our differences and were becoming stronger and stronger.

Chichi was able to get her parents a residency through her citizenship, but once they arrived, everything started going downhill. It was a nightmare. Her father didn't "accept" me, thus not allowing our friendship to continue. I find it interesting to this day that all of these people in her life who didn't even know me knew they didn't like me. I assumed they heard negative words about me somewhere that made them disapprove of me, even though I was the only one who helped his daughter in her most desperate times of need. I supported Chichi 100% for almost five years and never got so much as a "thank-you."

With this new disapproval, everything I built with Chichi was disappearing in the blink of an eye... for me only. She took a step back without any communication or explanation. I knew her family would continue to build wealth, success, and freedom, and she would no longer need anything from me. That was her ultimate goal, I think. Taking me out of her life seemingly meant nothing at all.

I saw it happening, but I didn't fully believe it. Or maybe, I just didn't want to. I had faith that she wasn't that cruel. As someone who had always fought for her, defending her to my friends and family, I hoped for the same in return. It's possible that this was a turning point that helped me feel unworthy once again.

> "In the end, we will not remember the words of enemies, but the silence of our friends." - M.L.K., Jr.

I tried to fight for our friendship, but eventually I stopped. I wanted to be loved and respected not because I fought for it, but because she wanted to respect and love me. I was hopeful that the day I stopped trying so hard would be the day she'd pick up the fight - the day she'd realize that I was slipping away from her life. However, it became clear that she'd intended to let go of our friendship earlier than I ever realized, or maybe, she'd never felt the same as me about it at all.

My last message to her was one where I humbly displayed my broken heart. It was left on "read."

While I know people grow apart, they disagree, fight, decide to leave each other's lives, I will never understand how someone can end a relationship with another person without discussing the "why." I truly believe no one deserves what happened to me in that scenario - I let a stranger into the lives of me and my kids. I took care of her. I helped her work to achieve her goals, sometimes putting more effort toward her goals than toward my own.

I felt a lot of pain during this time, but much of it was for my kids. Chichi played an integral role in their upbringing; they truly loved her. For her to leave without so much as a goodbye meant they experienced what it felt like to have someone walk out on them.

People often say respect and loyalty is earned, making you think you are in control of how others treat you. In reality, if someone ever does something to another person that goes against your values, they can just as easily do the same to you. Remember that no matter what you do for others, they are the only ones who are in control of how they treat you.

When people do you wrong, do good anyway. Show gratitude always. Know that someone else's success is not your failure. At any given time, people who are important to you can walk away from your life. Let them do that before you ever dim your light to make them feel more comfortable.

Chapter 29

Raising strangers

"Teaching kids how to count is okay, but teaching them what counts is rare." - Agnieszka Sycewicz

Sometimes, we develop friendships that will last us our entire lifetime, and we hardly ever realize it while it's happening. It's important that we continue to meet new people over time, but it's also important to consider those who can remain in our lives with love and understanding. While it may be easy to call someone a "best friend" and relate to them on a daily basis, it's more rare to be able to see the importance of a person's presence within a single moment.

As I continued raising my boys, one of my biggest goals was to make sure they could go to the best school I could afford. Again working two jobs, day and night, I took all the money I made and put it toward tuition for my kids. Sometimes, this meant we didn't have lights for them to see their homework, but if I had any say, they'd be staying in school.

I learned over time that being a mother of three, especially when one of my kids started having behavior challenges, it wasn't enough just to know generally how to raise them - what to do and not do. It was so much more than that, and I needed help. I sought guidance for my son who was having difficulty, and by the grace of God, I unknowingly found that guidance in the blessing of a human that was Ms. Meli. After being in our lives for only a short while, I knew she was one of the most amazing teachers I'd ever meet.

Ms. Meli was a math teacher who is an extraordinary human full of spirit and hope and devoid of judgment. She quickly became a friend of mine and spent lots of time helping to support my kids' growth, which helped me so immensely. I realize now that I never shared my most sincere gratitude with her, as sometimes I didn't see what she did for us as anything more than what teachers were "supposed" to do.

I know now that she went so far above and beyond for my family. The love and care she offered my boys was more than I could have ever asked for. Keeping them in a private school was something I struggled with so much; I could barely take my kids to school some days let alone spend time with them on their homework. Yet Ms. Meli helped to bring light into their lives.

Today my kids are grown, and over a decade after first meeting her, we are all a family. She remains in our lives and continues to make a positive impact on my kids as a teacher, friend, and someone who will always guide them in the direction of success.

Ms. Meli - if I never said it out loud, I'm saying it now. The biggest thank you for helping to raise my kids in a way I couldn't will live forever in these pages. I know the money I put toward their schooling didn't just get them an education, it got them knowledge of life and a true friendship that they can carry with them forever.

Chapter 30

The Unexpected Blessing

"No one has ever done it alone." - Grant Cardone

Placing my kids into a private school, the Montessori Children's House, was more than I could handle. I can remember many moments where I felt so embarrassed, whether I was running late to drop them off in the mornings or to pick them up in the evenings. Sometimes by the time I pulled into the parking lot, the school was completely closed - lights off and everything. My boys would sit outside the school door waiting, probably all the while wondering if I was going to show up. That situation wasn't preferable to me as a mom, but there was little I could do to change it. I worked my day job at the spa from 9 a.m. - 5 p.m., rushed to the school to pick them up before it closed at 6 p.m., and then brought everyone home to get dinner and prepare for my night shift as a waitress, which went from 11 p.m. - 6 a.m. I came home each morning exhausted, practically sleepwalking half the time, but ready to do it all over again. It just meant that occasionally, we ran late.

No matter what it took, I was determined to keep my boys in that school, and being able to do it successfully made me so proud, even if I dropped them off at 7 in the morning and wasn't able to pick them up until 7 at night (FYI: school ended at 3; the after-school childcare program ended at 6).

The reason I felt so embarrassed was because it seemed like the life I was living and creating for my sons wasn't the same kind of life other parents at that school were living and creating. For a long time, my boys were the only ones waiting outside after 6... until one day, when I saw another mother arrive at the same time I did. God has a mysterious way of putting people into our lives for a reason, doesn't He? I started seeing this mom pick up her kids late every day, and it felt like a huge weight had been lifted. Seeing two other boys sitting next to mine made me feel less sad and guilty. After that, I knew I wasn't alone.

Late pick up nights turned into reasons for us to converse with each other, each sharing that we were single moms working hard to do the best we could for our boys. Our casual hellos in the parking lot lead to minutes, then hours of chatting. Months and then years later, we were still bonding over this shared experience of being the moms who are always late to pick up their kids.

We were two imperfect mothers, trying to be perfect for everyone else but realizing we could be our true selves with each other. Subconsciously, we were building a friendship without really being alike in any other way. Sharing our dreams and goals became a parking lot routine, and without even knowing it, those conversations helped each of us make steps toward them.

Every setback I encountered as a mother, in my career, or even in my love life, I confided in her. I trusted her as a guide and mentor on the road to my success. We had different perspectives on these things, but we stood by each other through the challenges each of us experienced.

A single mom who inspired me with harsh conversations about my life choices and how they impact my family, the "simple" sales girl working for Comcast became a realtor over the years. All the while, she continued helping me grow toward my success as well.

She still stands by my side today, a guiding angel for me and someone who helps me to be a better woman, friend, and most importantly, mother. She is the biggest reason for the changed person I am today - the person who makes deliberate choices for the futures of myself and my children.

Some women see other women as competition. In the past, that's how I have been, but that was never how this mom was at all. She reminded me that figuring out who we are is critical; and sometimes, first figuring out who we are not is the key. Together, we each became the fuel to light the fires in our lives. I watched her growth and learned so much from her compassion and kindness. Here was this woman who started as a complete stranger to me, but gave so much care and support without any expectation. I tried my best to be this person in life as well, and that's how I knew that even though our personalities were opposite, our souls were the same. I will forever be grateful that we were each late to pick up our kids.

A special thank you for always being the person who sees the winner in me, for always pushing me to reach my greatest potential, and guiding me every step of the way towards my victory!

Forever blessed to have you in my life.

Chapter 31

"The bartender"

Searching for validation

"You are enough."

After having had three serious relationships that didn't quite work out as planned, I decided I was no longer looking for love. In my mind, I was done; I wanted to be free.

The thing was, I had never really experienced being single since I was a teenager. This meant my new choice to embrace the single life didn't last all that long.

Subconsciously, I began to resent every guy who had shown up in my life. In my eyes and in the eyes of others, I started acting like a man, forgetting how to be the woman I was meant to be. I was cruel and careless, dating without measuring any consequences. I can say today that during that period of my life, I dated so many men at the same time that they became who I was. I got non-stop attention any time, anywhere; it was almost as if I was in a relationship with someone that I just met - constantly. No matter how much time I spent with them, whether it was a one-night stand or a few days, they never wanted to leave me. I felt so much power knowing so many men wanted me, knowing they wanted to be with and talk to me all of the time.

What made me feel even more powerful was knowing how to play the game. I had learned so much about men over the years that I was able to use everything I had experienced to "win the game" - without anyone but me knowing it was a game at all. But what did I really want to achieve by winning? I might have been gaining back some of the validation I lost along my path, but it was damaging me even more as receiving it from my circle of men became an addiction.

Getting to know a man and studying his behavior became my weapons for future payback, without me realizing I was really only hurting myself. In doing this, I couldn't fall in love. I couldn't love anyone. Every man that I met became temporary medicine to heal my pain from the past. As I continued my night life as a cocktail waitress, I came across him - the one and only - "The Bartender."

When I first met him, I knew he was different. He had a unique way about him that made a person feel like they were special. After working together for a while, I started to see him with different eyes. It wasn't love at first sight, but my attraction to him got stronger and stronger over time. Knowing he spent each night with a different girl meant I knew he was someone I didn't need complicating my life, but I wasn't a saint either. Initially, both of us were so focused on other people and our own craziness that we didn't believe anything would ever happen between us - especially since we knew each other solely from work. Sometimes we would close the club together at the end of the night, and after a while this led to drinking and chatting afterward. Next thing I knew, I was going home with him.

It really shouldn't have surprised me all that much; it was a classic repeat of my usual story. A player who had as many girls as he wanted was my go-to. No matter who I was dating, I always ended up in his arms. Years passed like this and I still couldn't stop seeing him. I always asked myself, "Why him?" In my eyes, the Bartender started out as a pawn for me, but I realized later that he was playing the same game.

It was ideal for both of us, though, I think - that set up. We never really spent any romantic time together; it was just party after party, he was with other girls and I was with other guys. It was all going well until one morning, I woke up with feelings for him. I wanted to date him, despite knowing at my core that that would never happen. I was finally losing the game I had been winning at for so long. He was a better player. It was painful, but maybe payback for all the hearts I had broken since I started.

Even though we shared the nightlife, our lifestyles didn't align. I had kids and attachments; I was not free. He had nothing tying him down, and he wanted to keep it that way. Thus, when my emotions got involved, I knew I had to run before I ended up broken again. Except, I couldn't. I couldn't forget or leave him; it felt like I didn't know how.

After quite some time, he asked me out on a date. I was speechless; it almost felt like I could set my feelings aside and take the lead in the game. Excited and nervous, despite the time we had spent under his sheets, I was ready for the perfect first date. I went to the club, and as I arrived, I saw him seated with another woman. I told myself to be strong, to remember the game. As I introduced myself to the woman, a third woman appeared. Then a fourth, and so on. Apparently, all he wanted was to take a bunch of pretty girls to the club and shine.

I went along with it, not knowing the whole time that all the other women also thought they were going to be the only ones with him on the date. Like I said, he had a way of making you feel special. To me though, I was still different from those other women. It wasn't just in my imagination either; no matter how many other people were there, surrounding him, flirting with him, I was the one he went home with. God knows he had choices, but so did I, and he knew that. Whatever he did toward me, I did right back.

Despite his player persona, the Bartender was actually an exceptional gentleman. He was so caring and transparent, but he couldn't (or maybe didn't want to) offer me the loyalty I was looking for from him. Therefore, I continued following his lifestyle, having to face the fact that there was an extremely low chance of finding stability in our "booty-call relationship." Over time, the way he was living became the way I lived; I almost became the woman version of him. I had my freedom and saw other men whenever I wanted, but still went home to him no matter what.

I got to the point where I trusted him and didn't think he would ever betray me. I'm not sure where this belief came from, as he never showed a sign of faithfulness during any of our encounters. On a night out with Chichi (before we had a falling out), we ran into the Bartender and he invited me to go to his house. I decided to let Chichi come along, as we were inseparable at the time. I didn't think it would be a big deal for her to sleep on his couch.

I could picture him breaking boundaries with strangers, because that's what he always did and we didn't have a title. However, I did not see it coming that he would get with my friend. She was a person I loved and trusted, but as I came back from the bathroom, I saw them together. At that moment, I hated her, but I was more disappointed in him. Why?

As quickly as I declared hate, I forgave them. I went back to my friendship with Chichi and tried to bury the memory. I trusted her more than anyone, and I felt betrayed. I focused on myself: Did I do something wrong to cause this? I cried and overthought everything. Doubt crept in and my self-esteem - something I had been trying to build - plummeted. I developed a jealousy of Chichi that I couldn't quite explain.

That night never repeated itself and I moved on in my actions, but my heart was still secretly broken. The amount of pain I felt then and still feel toward that night is how I know I loved the Bartender, how I know I lost the twisted game we had been playing together for over six years.

I learned more about men during my time with him than I had ever learned before, and that itself meant I had learned lessons that will never be forgotten. Many men have had an important role in my life, and some still do to this day. He was one of those men who left a mark.

People often say that in order to recover from a broken heart, you have to find another love. That was the pattern I continued to repeat, and it reinforced the idea that I couldn't heal on my own.

Was the game I created in my head just a temporary escape from my hectic life, or did I truly believe I had healed from all my broken love stories and could continue living in that way?

Was I trying hard enough to heal? Or was it just easier for me not to dig deep down to all the imperfections that I had buried?

Chapter 32

Healing

We all have memories we like to revisit that help us smile when we're feeling hurt. Some people don't like looking back on the past because in doing so, they are reminded that not every memory is that kind of memory.

When our memories still hurt us, we have not fully healed. Many times, instead of working toward healing, we cover up our traumas, which allows us to repeat them with new characters or mistakes. However, when we do this, we always end up feeling the same pain. Repeating the hurt doesn't help us, but rather, leaves us feeling more broken than ever before.

Chapter 33

"El tigre"

"Love can be magic. But magic can sometimes just be an illusion" - Javan

Without being fully healed, I continued on the only way I knew how: slowly moving to another chapter of love. It was a feeling I couldn't resist. I created our love story the second I met my next man, blindly claiming he was "the one."

Young, good looking, dark, on vacation in Miami from New York City. He was a guy from my dreams, and he was finally here. I had waited for a feeling as unique as that ever since things ended with Lagos, almost ten whole years prior. In essence, he was my Lagos 2.0. I'd had years of different love stories in my life but this one, this man, was one of a kind. The feeling in my soul was so undeniable, and I recognized it immediately because I had only felt it one other time in my existence - with Lagos. While I knew that meant it was true, I also meant it would be very hard to be rid of.

Meeting this man for the first time made my broken heart temporarily fade. I was standing in line at a club with Chichi when he grabbed my hand and said, "Come with me, I have a table." I said, "Let's go!" ...How insane can a person be to say, after that brief of an interaction, "He is the one for me"? Not many people. Perhaps only me?

That same night, we ended up in each other's arms in his hotel room. It was actually ideal; he was with his cousin and I was with Chichi. A fun night turned into breakfast the next morning, then we spent another night and day together until he had to return to New York. That quick weekend morphed into many memories of the amazing time the two of us spent together over years.

We all called him "El Tigre"; he was a fast thinker and very sharp. He had big dreams and goals, and I admired him for that. He wanted kids. He spoke with such a passion for conquering the world that I had been blinded by awe again - even more than I ever had been before.

The time spent with him was the first time in my life that I regretted my choice to not have more kids. I kept thinking of him; I woke up each morning thinking of him and every man I met paled in comparison. I was obsessed with him in the most sick and obsessive way a human can be. It most definitely all started as fantasy, but I desperately wanted that fantasy to become my reality. I dreamt that one day, I would finally get that fairytale "happy ending." I placed my life on hold just so I could see him anytime he desired. He would visit me, I began to visit him, and this all went on for years. All the while, I wouldn't give anyone else the slightest chance to get close to me. The more time I spent with him, the more I fell for him. I was ready to do whatever it took to win his heart. As my friend, La Tati would say, "It takes courage to go through this again!"

As I continued to live in a world of fantasy, I began searching for someone to take the feelings for El Tigre away... all the while knowing I didn't truly want that to happen. Once again, I was creating paths in my life that didn't align with my reality, and no one could stop me.

I think we've established by now that I'm a bit of a dreamer. When I dream, I dream with my whole being. So I welcomed this man into my life like I had done with other men before, dreaming of the day he decided to commit to me.

CHAPTER 34

LESSONS ARE REPEATED UNTIL THEY ARE LEARNED

As sad as it sounds, I was no longer looking for anything more than fun with men. I promised myself that I would not create any more fantasies, no more fairy tales or imaginary love stories. No more heart breaks. I knew I needed to heal in order to welcome someone permanently into my life, so I avoided second dates, second phone calls, anything that would enable me to fall for someone before I felt ready.

It's funny how our stories find a way of repeating themselves, even if we don't understand why at the time. I truly believe that lessons in life will be repeated until they are learned!

You'd think that after everything I had been through, I would have learned my lesson, but one night at the bar, while I was asking for a drink and grieving my unsuccessful love story with El Tigre, there he was. A man behind the bar and I started flirting, but minutes later he revealed that he was married.

That was a big "hell no" moment. I had done many things I wasn't not proud of, but one thing I had always stayed away from was married guys. Maybe the fact that I was once married stayed with me, as I was cheated on during that time. I know for a fact that it's one of the hardest recoveries for a woman (or a man, I'd suppose, but I can only speak from a woman's perspective here).Entering this chapter of my life was about protecting myself at all costs, so seeing someone who was married seemed like it could be exactly what I was looking for. Maybe I should give it a try, I told myself... Maybe this is a guy who won't call me again. After all, why would he? He is married. In that moment, I made a choice, choosing to have a night of fun.

The attention this man gave me was unique. There was kindness, you could almost feel his warm and genuine heart. However, I looked away, avoiding what I could already see down the road. Our one-night stand turned to the next day, then to the next day, then to weeks, and later, months.

Was I surprised? Maybe But deep down, I was simply repeating my same, destructive pattern again. Only this time, it was with a married man. Why had I decided to turn one night into many? Our story had the most difficult beginning for me, but it just flowed as if we had known each other forever.

I was used to so much drama, jealousy, abuse, games, and betrayal, but this was different. While the first three months weren't easy (because he would go back to his wife), it didn't totally bother me. I was able to live a life on my own terms. However, it didn't take long before we were living together.

He was five years younger than me, and had built five years of marriage with his wife. He had no kids despite desperately wanting them. Even though he knew I couldn't give him kids of his own, he made the choice to walk away from his marriage and start a life with me and my three boys. During his divorce, he was hesitant, wondering if he made the right choice. I didn't blame him for that at all.

His family didn't approve of us, which made things even more difficult. In their eyes, an older woman coming in with three kids, firm against not having kids with him, and breaking apart his marriage was like one hell after another.

When it comes down to it, the two of us were friends unlike any other relationship I've had with another man. The whole world was against us, but we had each other. I was his strength, the one helping him to turn his life around. I was there to pick him up and push him toward his full potential, which was all I could do to begin to make up for what I couldn't give him. Out of guilt, I put the things I wanted out of life aside to help him achieve his goals... and he did.

This may sound strange, but I can truly say this was one of the healthiest relationships I had ever been in.

We had been living together for four years, but I still wasn't healed from my prior relationships. I couldn't forget or let go of the past. Being unable to let go meant I was hurting him, and he felt my feelings whenever they came up. I shared everything with him; he was a true friend to me and someone I could share my deepest thoughts with.

At the same time, I was somehow waiting for the moment he would ask me to be his wife, something that I wasn't truly, internally ready for.

Maybe I wanted to be ready, but I was stuck on my past, big time. To cover up my weaknesses, I went looking for doctors who could help me reverse what I had done years ago. Maybe I would decide to give him the children he wanted. I was ready and willing.

But... no. I stopped myself. I knew I could not make a choice like that just because. I looked back at my life and realized I wanted more for my growth, more for my career. I knew I never wanted to struggle again.

His vision was different. His drive was not there, the comfort zone became his friend, and I was dragging him along, constantly pushing him in every aspect of his life. It became too much for him. I saw him trying so hard, but he just couldn't keep up. I was doing everything possible, but I was still on the elevator to success to give us a better life. We had plans to buy a home. It was like a dream was coming true. I was working and saving every dollar I could to be able to put a downpayment on a house. We found a place that we could afford, but as we were deciding whether to move to a new chapter in our life together, he had nothing to offer to help me get us there.

I didn't really know what to think. All I knew was that I had to let him go. We didn't want the same things and we couldn't keep going the way we were. It was by far the hardest decision I ever made when it came to my feelings and my romantic love for another person. So many of my decisions to leave people in the past were hard and painful but they had something in common: the people I was leaving had caused some sort of pain, disappointment, or betrayal in some form. Not him. He caused me no pain and did no damage to my life. He showed me how to calm down, how to be able to just sit and watch TV. He took care of me and the kids in the most genuine way possible, and that's something I will always be so grateful for.. I knew it was time to let him fulfill his dreams of having a family on his own, so I told him he could move on. I told him I would be all right, that I would give someone else a chance - even though that was a lie at the time.

In my entire history of break ups, I had never walked away from someone after saying our goodbyes with tears and pure love toward one another, until him.

I knew letting him go was the right thing to do for his life and what he wanted. Shortly after that, he had a baby boy with someone new. Meanwhile, I chose to remain single, focusing on my career and kids rather than putting myself into another love story that would only end.

The part I will forever miss about him is the friendship we built together. It was truly one of a kind.

"Every human being deserves to follow their dreams, even if their dreams aren't the same as yours."

In the end, he deserves the world.

Chapter 35

By the time they decide to support you, they will have to book you

"I am what I choose to become." - Carl Jung

When you learn to expect the unexpected, that's when miracles really happen. The journey of my career has truly been a blessing, filled with overcoming hate, insecurity, and people who wanted to harm me. Throughout everything, I kept working hard, believing that one day my dream of becoming a massage therapist would become a reality. This story starts when I was working as a beauty technician at a top spa in Miami.

After I graduated from the massage therapy program, I wasn't able to obtain my license. I tried taking the test three times and failed each time. This led to ultimate insecurities regarding my knowledge of the subject. But at the same time, I couldn't give up.

Years after graduation, I didn't know how I would ever be able to get my life together and study to retake the test. All I had was a diploma, which meant nothing for my career without the passing test result. Somehow though, I always chose whatever job I had at the time over preparing for something that could change my life for the better - maybe because of the instant financial benefit of adding more shifts.

One afternoon, something unexpected happened. One of my colleagues didn't show up for work, and the spa didn't have anyone to cover the massages for the day. My boss didn't see a way out of the mess, so she asked me to perform one of the scheduled massages. She was risking her job by doing this, but her trust in me was the beginning of a serious shift in my life. Because she took a chance on me, I decided to take a chance on myself.

What started from one staffing emergency led to outstanding feedback from guests, which led to my boss giving me more services. I got better and better, and our top clientele began requesting me. Telling people of that caliber that I "wasn't available" meant telling them something they really didn't want to hear. Then, to tell them the reason I couldn't perform their massage was because I wasn't licensed was even worse! So, the spa let me keep doing them, which was the start of my career but was threatening to some of my coworkers.

I started to get comfortable in the job. I was getting booked for massage after massage, to the point where I was no longer available to perform the services I was actually certified and hired to do. After years of working basically under the table and feeling like there was no way out, I was finally given the opportunity to achieve. While I considered my coworkers friends, once I started doing more massages, I was envied. They began to hate me, experiencing jealousy because of the unfairness of it all. Here I was, practicing without a license, taking over clients they had lost. They had no mercy for the fact that I was a single mom, trying to do everything I could to take care of my kids. The situation felt like it was out of my control.

I was doing the best I could to be good at my job, constantly in fear of getting caught. I was pulled aside by an employee at the spa who informed me that I had "friends" who were doing what they could to make sure I never massaged again. At the same time, I felt immense pressure to prove to my boss that she made the right choice, that I was worth her risk.

The next day, I called my boss and said I had decided to take a month-long leave of absence. I said, "Give me one month and I will do whatever it takes to pass this exam," even when leaving meant losing all of my income, which I could not afford to do. That was that. I opened the books ten years after graduating. It was like I had to start again from the beginning. I left my kids with no electricity, eating rice and eggs everyday for dinner while I was absent like never before, diving deeper into debt. I lost contact with every friend I had and missed birthdays and special events. I spent all my time staring at books and looking at my body, which I had painted just to learn every single muscle in the human body. Weeks passed by like this. Then, I received a phone call that someone had sent an inspector to book a massage with me at the spa, not knowing I wasn't working at the moment. It was as if God was protecting me. They couldn't get what they were after.

The day came for me to take the state exam. I hadn't slept for weeks, but I was finally doing it, and I passed. I went back to work with more power than I could ever have imagined, as there was nothing left for anyone to attack me with. My boss took me back, and as a result of my hard work, I became one of the top massage therapists in the spa industry.

Your current situation doesn't have to be the end result. I spent years hoping I would someday be where I am now. That's what I was believing in, the potential to achieve my dreams.

Chapter 36

Dreams Turn to Disaster

"Nothing is impossible."

I had achieved my goal of becoming a massage therapist, so my career was looking up. However, personally, I had ended my relationship just as I got ready to buy my first single-family home, and it needed a tremendous amount of work.

I had saved everything I could for the downpayment and had nothing left, so I couldn't afford to fix anything. I shared my story with a friend, and he reached out to another friend who offered to help with anything that needed fixing.

Knowing I wasn't in a great financial position, he offered for me to pay him back for the work he was doing on the house. I was excited, feeling so blessed. I couldn't believe everything he did - walls were torn apart, floors were redone, I mean, the whole house was as if it was about to be rebuilt.

The person working on the house said, "Don't worry, it will be done in no time! You'll be able to move in soon." Weeks after that, the "company" disappeared, and so did the person who said they would be fixing my house.

I was devastated. My home was absolutely destroyed and I had to pay the mortgage on it while we were homeless. I searched for a shelter for my family to live in in the meantime. My friends told me to forget about the house and go into foreclosure, but I couldn't give up. I got another job, then another, then another, as we rented out little rooms in other people's homes. All my kids were sleeping in one bed. This went on for 11 months, while I saved all I could to fix the house myself. It was such a financially-tasking ordeal - paying the mortgage on an empty house, paying to fix the empty house, and paying to rent other places to stay while the house was being fixed. I was so lucky that I had close friends to help with my kids, as I had to be away from them to work more than five jobs and chase as much money as possible.

After living in nine different places over the 11 months, we finally moved into our home. It wasn't perfect, but it was livable while I continued to fix it. Each of my kids got their own bed, and even though it was far from finished, I was in a place I could call my home.

I remember asking myself when this would all end. I wondered when things would stop being so terribly hard. Even though I truly believed everything happened for a reason, I was ready for the reason to be revealed.

I decided I needed to really buckle down. It was finally clear to me, after everything with the house, that I had to turn my life around, focusing all of my energy on myself and my kids. No more dating - time to work on my career and my success. After going deeper into debt that I had ever gone, I began paying off my debts, slowly turning the nightmare into a beautiful story I could someday be proud to share.

That experience showed me who in my life I could count on. The mom from my kids' school parking lot who became a realtor? Her name was Caroline. She was the one who helped me find my first home, and that was only the beginning of the connections and help she gave to me over time. As I became close with the team of people who finished my house, I decided to enroll myself in school for construction, to become a general contractor - I know, what a motivation! I had no idea what I was doing at first, but eventually opened a construction company on my own. It was a wild ride, as recommendations from the realtor were coming at us right and left. I officially became a subcontractor, making contracts for people to do their work. The team that worked on my house was phenomenal, and I met more and more people in the field through that. Work was getting done; there were no disappointments, nor fear. I was learning as I was going through it, surprising myself every day.

Chapter 37

Life Jeopardy

"You can't have a rainbow without a little rain." - Unknown

While working a full-time job at the spa and a part-time job in the spa industry as a whole, I decided to finally go after a new dream. Since I was pregnant with my oldest son, I'd wanted to participate in a bodybuilding competition as a bikini competitor. I started to train everyday at three in the morning, came home to get the boys ready for school, and then headed out to work on all of the projects I had going on.

My mind was in the bodybuilding sphere, but my body started shifting in a different direction. I was told I needed a severe surgery as soon as possible. The risks of not undergoing the operation included losing my leg.

I was feeling like I couldn't be knocked down any more! This was a new nightmare. How was I supposed to handle recovering from a surgery like this when I had so many things to do and so much to make up for? I asked every person I knew to lend me money, with the goal of being able to get through the recovery time. Unfortunately, no one was able to help.

In tears, I confided in my friend, who decided to lend me some of her dad's money without his knowledge. I put everything I had going for me on pause, brought the kids to their dad's, and got ready for the unknown.

La Tati, my best friend, accompanied me on the journey out of the country for my surgery. There I was, in a hospital bed, left with total uncertainty. I didn't know what was going to happen with my body or overall health. Will I wake up with both my legs? Will I make it out alive?

Seven hours later, the operation was complete and I was both alive and with two legs. Despite the circumstances, I was signing contracts for other projects in my hospital bed. I was at a point where nothing was going to stop me.

As I began to recover, I had to put my training and the idea of competing on pause. When I came back to the States, I quit the general contractor program and the construction work and focused on gaining more clients as a massage therapist.

I applied to every spa around, working 12 hours a day if not more. I was unstoppable - tired or not, weekends or not. I was working to pay back the money from when I was recovering, the money for fixing my house, and the money for all my general debts. I was at my breaking point, nearly $100,000 in debt with shattered credit, and I refused to go backward, ever. No matter what obstacles presented themselves, I was going to persevere.

Chapter 38

Planet Collapse

We all can understand what happened in the world in March of 2020. There was a global pandemic. We were all left with no work and extreme fear for what each new day would bring.

There was a lot of sadness going on around the world, but nothing was scary or sad enough to keep me still. I had so many calluses on my heart and my brain; no one was going to tell me to put my life on pause.

I started looking into where I could go, what I could do, and how I could keep providing for my family. There was financial help on the way for many, but that wasn't sure enough or secure enough for me.

I decided to reach out to everyone I knew and ask if anyone wanted to have massage services done at home, despite the fact that almost no one wanted visitors. Many people were scared at the thought of me (or anyone else) going into their homes.

Regardless of how scared they were, I sat down and created a massage business for myself... one where I was the only employee. Most of the world was shut down; people stayed home out of fear. Differently, I was on the streets every day looking for opportunities, even where there were curfews. I refused to sit still and wait for permission to move.

Just like that, one client turned to a few clients. Then, recommendations started coming in unexpectedly, with a high demand for my services. I was increasing my prices as days went by, and the clientele I surrounded myself with didn't mind paying. For the first time in my life, I felt like I could breathe again; the outside noise was silent to me. It wasn't necessarily that my brain didn't capture the reality of the world, but I was hyper focused on the light at the end of my personal tunnel.

I was almost considering resigning from my job when they decided to reopen the spa. I was the first one they spoke with about coming back. Honestly, I had been doing better on my own in times of uncertainty. However, I decided to go back anyway.

While expanding my business, I couldn't keep up with the demands of the services requested. I was just about to declare that I didn't want to do it anymore. I started looking for mentors who could help me make the best decision about which way to go.

Once things slowly started normalizing again, a live event was held in Miami that I decided to attend: the 10X Growth Conference.

As a thank you to my realtor friend, Caroiline. I surprised her with a ticket to attend the seminar with me. She was the one who introduced me to the videos and workshops from Grant Cardone during the pandemic, so I thought it was only fitting. It was also such a good feeling, remembering where I started and realizing

I was actually able to spend thousands of dollars on a gift for someone else. It was priceless.

The experience was definitely an eye opener. We shared our ideas, dreams, and goals, and talked about how far we had come. Sitting in the car after the event, my friend and I went over our plans. She stopped me and said, "You are now in the driver's seat of your business and career. You need to let go of driving and become a passenger." Wow, I thought to myself. I had no idea how I would be able to let go of everything I built, or if I'd then just be waiting to see it all disappear.

The next morning, I reached out to people I trusted - people with no jobs - and offered them a spot on my team. In doing so, I created a mobile massage company where I was no longer the only employee. Many of the people I reached out to said yes, and just like that, my solo massage business became a business that created jobs for others. I no longer had to break my back or turn clients away who needed my services.

Over the course of a few months, I generated more money than I had working multiple jobs in a year during such difficult times for humanity... while still working my full-time job that served me for other things in life. During those times when everyone was getting into debt to survive, I was getting out of every debt I ever had.

I wanted to take my success in another direction and finally become financially free. I found within me another goal, which was to become a real estate investor. I created another business for myself and became who I chose to become.

Having turned my life around, I was hungrier and more committed than ever. I found an opportunity as the real estate market heightened, only to find out I had a good amount of equity in my home. There I was, fighting for a chance to have the best come-back in history. Due to the pandemic, there were many obstacles and struggles that made it harder than usual, but in the middle of a worldwide crisis, I was able to close on my home, which left all my debts paid off and all equity in cash in my bank account.

As strange and sad as it is to say, the first year of the pandemic was the best year of my life. I was able to dream with reality in mind, without the nightmare of illusion. While it would be easy and (finally) safe to keep all my money in a bank account, that route wasn't for me. Feeling stronger than ever, I looked for ways to reinvest everything I had worked for.

With help and guidance from my amazing realtor friend, I had another successful purchase of an investment property. I started to fix it from scratch, this time with no partners. I put everything I earned into that house, and three months later I had fixed, then flipped the property. I generated more money than I dreamt of earning in years at my main job.

All that being said, sometimes, the nightmares we go through are our best teachers in life. Without my first experience of abandoning a home and ending up homeless, I wouldn't have come close to becoming a real estate investor. We all have to find the hustler inside us, and we have to be willing to take risks and chance failure. What we learn along the way is that without persistence and consistency, we can't reach our true destination. We learn that no one can do it alone.

We all need people in our lives who will hold our hand when we need comfort, stop us when we need to breathe, and push us when we feel weak. However, if you can't start by depending on yourself, you'll just drift in circles for a long time... trust me, I know.

Chapter 39

The comeback

By this point, my life had more clarity than I could have ever imagined. After finally letting go of everything and everyone who no longer served a purpose, I embraced peace. I was finally on the right path - no more heart breaks, no more pain from the past. I spent most of my time working, as I preferred that to become my addiction over any other behavior of my past. Having any free time always got me in trouble, so I stayed busy and forgot how to be my past self.

I was still single, but was no longer searching for love. After years without contact with past flames, I randomly started receiving phone calls and messages from an ex-boyfriend - the one I was with when I first began working at the nightclub. I answered one of the calls, and after many chats about the past, we decided to see each other. He was single at the time with two sons of his own, and he desperately wanted me to meet them. I was in a really good place in my life so the past was all forgiven, and when we met we shared our memories with one another. It was revealed that his return to my life was to try to get me back. I went through a range of emotions learning this, but realized I was a completely different person when he knew me. I wasn't the same woman anymore. We decided not to pursue a relationship, and today we are at peace with one another. We can and still do talk, there's no bad blood, and I'm content to keep him as a friend because I know we can count on one another.

As if seeing him. wasn't enough to test my growth, two weeks later, I got a phone call from the Bartender after years of not speaking to one another. My head was still spinning while trying to understand the meaning of everything that was happening, but I went with the flow of life and agreed to meet him. On my way, past insecurities started to bubble to the surface as I remembered our history. When we saw each other, he acted differently, as if I was someone he had just met. We spent the evening together and it felt like what we had in our past was rekindled. I found myself in tears the next day - but this time, they were tears of happiness from the joy he had given me. I saw him again, hoping his acts were just another illusion I created so I could easily walk away. They weren't. He made my time with him the most magical I had ever experienced - with him or with anyone else to this point.

Though I enjoyed my time with the Bartender, I still carried love for Tigre. The pain resurfaced and I wasn't clear on my feelings. However, it didn't matter. The Bartender had to go back home - he had moved since we last knew each other - and I didn't know whether I'd see him again before his departure.

Two days later I was sitting at home, overthinking the magical moments the Bartender and I had spent together, when I looked down at my phone to a notification from El Tigre. He had just landed in Miami and wanted to see me.

I asked God, "What's happening in my life right now? This can't be - everyone returning at the same time with only a few days separating them?"

I was excited though, this was the guy. I had put everyone else on pause in the past with the hopes of being with him. When I went to see him, you can only imagine what was going on in my brain.

As I sat down with him for a drink, there was an empty feeling. I couldn't understand what changed, but I saw him with different eyes. I thought to myself, "What is really going on?" I had no idea. I stayed with him for the night, and when I returned home, all I did was cry.

I had no idea what to think about the fact that years of strong feelings of love and connection had disappeared. My tears were tears of sadness, but there was a bit of happiness too, happiness for finally being free of love.

His return had shown me how much I had grown. He remained the same guy I fell in love with years before, but I just didn't see what I saw in the past.

That month was full of moments with the three of them that closed every chapter of my bleeding wounds. Each of these men will forever have a special place in my heart, but today I'm free of pain. I can decide what I want for myself and choose who is worth being a part of my life.

Chapter 40

Back to Poland

"The weak can't forgive. Forgiveness is an attribute of the strong." - Mahatma Gandhi

As the year came to a close, I had so many emotions running through my mind. I knew there was one last thing I had to do: go back home to Poland, a place I hadn't visited since my dad died.

It was tough to be back there as the woman I am today. My purpose in visiting was to get as many answers as possible to the questions I'd been asking my whole life. I was in my home country looking for closure. I met with my mom and my sister together, and after not seeing them for so many years, it was awkward. We were all so different; it was as if they didnt know me and vice versa. As we sat at the dinner table, I asked questions and told secrets. I revealed what had gone unspoken for so long. I could tell they were surprised at my choices of words... I aimed to be humble and full of forgiveness. I shared my darkest thoughts and stories. My mother and sister gave me advice, which was to seek help, to figure out why I chose to forgive those who had hurt me, abused me, and abandoned me. They saw that quality in me as a weakness, something I needed to cure. I, however, saw it as my biggest blessing and greatest gift.

I went to Poland seeking the truth, and I think my family answered what they could to the best of their abilities. In the end, I got my peace, and they were left with the reality that I was no longer the "troubled" teenage girl they remembered.

Chapter 41

Circle of Friends

"This is just the beginning of where I'm headed, and I promise you, you will not be left behind."

This chapter is my very favorite because I get to give a shout out to some people who mean the world to me.

Sometimes, we have to cut people out of our lives for a reason, even if it's one we just seemingly made up in our heads. My biggest struggle until this point in my life was letting people go when I didn't think I had a "reason," i.e., when they had done me no "harm." However, going through life I realized that people don't have to necessarily harm you in order to no longer be serving your growth and potential. The people we keep in our lives should be those who see us for who we are *and* for who we can become, while supporting us along the journey from one to the other.

During my lifetime, I fought for a lot of validation. I tried to make everyone around me happy by always being available and catering to their every need as best I could. However, I didn't always feel like the people I was trying to make happy cared about me as much as I did them. Thus, I created my friendship circle, which I share with my friends to this day. This moved me forward on my path to clarity by helping me to identify where the people around me stood in my life. It took me 40 years to finally understand the importance of this, so I'm sharing it with you now in the hopes that some of you can get it earlier in life.

The circle is meant to place people where they belong based solely on *their actions*, not your feelings. Instead of cutting everyone off based on goal or vision differences, I did my homework and placed everyone in my life where they belonged in my circle.

The beauty of the circle is that it is infinite; meaning people can move freely up or down a level depending on changes that occur. It also makes it very clear as to when someone needs to be let go.

When I was considering the people I needed to add to my circle, I thought back on some serious friendships that have changed the course of my life. The first one I will mention is La Tati, the friend who has shown up in big ways at various points throughout this book. I met him when I was young and pregnant with my third son. He started out as just a regular guy that I met through work, but it was so easy to be his friend. I remember first introducing him to my husband at the time and trying so hard to prove he didn't like me. Little did I know that our small talk at work would lead to long conversations over the phone, coffee meet-ups, or him becoming a part of my family. His energy from the very start showed me that I met someone who could be a mentor I secretly searched for.

La Tati is so incredible; his character and loyalty are unmatched. He has been there through every struggle since I first met him and sometimes I ask myself if I'm even good enough to be his friend. He is my go-to for advice during the messier parts of life; I've called him to ask if I'm making the "right" decision on so many occasions. Anytime I'm uncertain, he is who I look to for guidance. Over the years, I've truly begun to view him as my savior; during my darkest days when I wanted to take my life, he was there to help me find the light.

You never have to ask La Tati for help, he just shows up. He knows exactly when to call and what to say; he is my hero.

La Tati has had to listen to a lot of bullshit over the years. Though not always, quite often he disagreed with my choices and gave me brutal advice but always kept walking beside me. I often wondered why. I felt like for such a long time that I couldn't offer him anything compared to what he had given me.

He reached a point where he had to leave the country to take care of his mother, who was sick. We had no idea how long his absence would be, and after he left I entered very dark places in life. During those moments, despite all he was doing to care for his family, he still answered my calls. Once he came back to the States, I was a mess, and probably had turned into a person he didn't recognize. He carried on with his love anyway. Fifteen years have passed and even though we have lived completely different lives, his transparency and friendship are just as strong today as when we met.

Now, I can move around any story of my life at will, but if I delete the memories with La Tati, everything else will be erased. Now that I am in a better place in life, I am eager to give back to him all that he ever gave to me. Today I strive for success, not only for myself and my kids, but for him. I strive for success so I can be the friend he deserves. I truly believe this is just the beginning for me, but no matter what, the triumph of my victories will be ours to share.

The biggest win in my life up to this point has been having him in my life.

> "Friends are hidden treasures that, over time, become our family." - Agnieszka Sycewicz

La Negra - where do I even begin?

This man is truly one in a million. I met him through La Tati, and he therefore already held a special place in my heart because of that. They were long-lost friends from home, and meeting him was priceless. He was so clearly unique from the moment he entered my life. We became best friends the day we met, without even questioning anything. He was someone who was constantly physically present, ready to play a crucial part in my memories.

During almost each chapter of this book, he was there. I think if I took the time to write all that we've been through together, I would run out of pages. At the time, he was like my husband, I just didn't sleep with him.

La Negra is truly loved by everyone. He knows how to make people laugh when they are in the midst of tragedy and lights up each room he walks into. He was a part of my dating life, my career, the lives of my friends, and the lives of my kids. Over a decade and a half he gave endless support - financial and emotional - when I was struggling with debts or just wanted to go out and have fun.

His ability to help people not only changed many of my harsh situations, but the situations of those around him. He was very specific about who he let enter his life, so I'm forever grateful that he chose me. I welcomed him into my life as if he were my family. Today we live different lives; we no longer have the nights out together or the crazy times we used to, but we are still standing and loving as the family we were created to be. Similar to my duties for La Tati, my duties for La Negra today are not only my continued loyalty to his friendship, but also my continued growth toward a reward that I will be sure he gets from me once I reach my final destination.

> "True friendship comes when the silence between two people is comfortable." - David Tyson

Laurita was a girl who worked with me at the spa. We were initially colleagues more than anything else; the blessing in this was that working together was a chance to see each other often. Our friendship grew slowly but very securely. She was someone I could go to with all my crazy stories day in and day out, and she always listened before giving me words of wisdom. At times, it felt as though I had no wisdom to give back to her. She was my council and I trusted her. She was there to guide me even when I didn't want to be guided. After 15 years, we no longer work together, but our friendship still exists. Now, we have a deeper love for one another, and to me, it feels less like a one-way street in terms of being able to offer value. I now feel like I can contribute words of wisdom and a helping hand, just like she has always offered me.

"The highest gratitude of my success is acknowledgment of your existence." - Agnieszka Sycewicz

Aura was another colleague whom I had the privilege of knowing. She was a huge factor in my success. I know she was secretly hated for giving me a helping hand in the past. Earlier, I shared a story of when I couldn't show my skills in my workplace, much less make money from them. Aura gave me an opportunity, not only to grow in my career but in my confidence. She helped me to shine. She was the reason my kids had food on the table when I came home from work, the reason I was able to work five jobs and still have hers to go to the next day - even when I was barely conscious and completely exhausted. She gave me rest when I needed it. During all the years of my messy life, she never held me back.

Our boss-employee relationship became a friendship filled with compassion and care. Therefore, I want to take space here to acknowledge her presence in my life and the importance of her role during my toughest times.

Aura's kindness was given to me just because; she didn't know all about the life I dealt with behind the scenes. I'm grateful to her for what she did for me, but also for the impact her kindness made on the lives of my kids.

"People come to your life for a reason."

After ending things with my bestie, I opened the door to another girl I had known for many, many years, but had never encountered as a "friend." It was the beginning of many friendships that I gained because of her persistence.

Lola was a single girl traveling around the world, and I joined her journey anytime I possibly could. We visited many countries and had a lot of fun together. She marked the beginning of my ability to interact with other women and to experience different outcomes for woman-woman friendships than what my past dictated. She was always surrounded by beautiful women and was an extremely secure woman herself. Honestly, sometimes it was a challenge to be around her, just to try to comprehend the freedom she had regarding herself and her confidence - something I struggled with all my life. The short vacations with her brought in a different perspective for how I see women in my own life today. Her friendship helped to bring a wave of healing for resentments I felt toward women in my past. Lola was the main reason that I was blessed enough to meet so many other wonderful women and build friendships with them.

I will always thank her for being someone with a natural ability to share the people or information she knows without any hesitations.

> "No matter how far we are in body, we will always be close in spirit."

During those travel times I was beyond blessed enough to meet Dominika who had a kind heart and pure soul that I could see from the very beginning. We bonded quickly, and lucky for me, she moved to Miami. As we both got to know each other, sharing our struggles and successes, we became very close. Years have gone by since we first met, yet she remains an important person in my life whom I consider to be a true friend. As I mentioned in my chapters before this, when you accept that a.) your friends do not have to be living on the same path as you and b.) you may not always be the friends who see each other every day, you realize the true importance of each other's presence. That is who Dominika is for me and I may be for her - a person who isn't seen every day, but will be the light during times of darkness.

> "Give a chance to a stranger and capture a lifelong friend." - Agnieszka Sycewicz

Sofia was a person I believe had been brought into my life for a very specific reason. Meeting her was a challenge of acceptance on my part, as she so much reminded me of a friend I had lost. She looked like Chichi, and her situation at the time was very similar. For this reason, I initially kept my distance; I was afraid to repeat the same story I had encountered before. However, she persisted to get to know me even though she didn't live in Miami. Despite feeling my resistance to getting to know her on a deeper level, she still showed up in my life or in my kids' lives. She made intentional plans to spend time with me. Unfortunately, she was willing to pay the price of my rejection, which was based in fear.

It wasn't Sofia's fault that her current situation was very much like Chichi's, and her actions on a daily basis slowly but surely led me to gain some trust for her. She understood my fear and past hurt, and never gave up trying to foster our friendship.

As time passed, I was there to mentor her and guide her in the right direction, just like I had done in the past with others. In the back of my mind, there was always a whisper not to get too close to her, that she would leave as soon as I helped her succeed. That whisper was one of fear and insecurity, a constant reminder of someone I loved who walked away from me after she got what she wanted.

Today we are really close, and the goals she accomplished with my help didn't cause her to leave me behind. My work for her life is being rewarded to this day, as her presence in *my* life is exceptional. She is genuinely concerned for and cares about me and my kids, and that is beyond what I can ask for a friend to offer.

What I learned from my past and applied when building this friendship was this: Honesty, as brutal as it can be, helps to grow friendships that are not rooted in fear. Because I was able to be transparent with Sofia about my pain, I was able to move past what had happened with Chichi and gain a truly wonderful friend.

"When you know, you know."

Lisa was one of those people you can't really figure out, but knowing her as the mother of my kids' friend as well as a long-time friend of Ms. Meli and my late pick-up realtor friend Caroiline,was enough for me to give a relationship with her a chance. In the beginning, it was strange, as there were secrets we both kept to protect the identities we had created over the years.

However, the first time we interacted as friends rather than as mothers was definitely telling. It was almost like we were the same... but we weren't?

The time we spent together made it feel like time didn't even exist. Hours of getting to know each other felt like seconds. It was like we had known each other our whole lives. Spending time together was just so natural. It hasn't been long since we decided to share those initial secrets with one another, but it has been a hell of a journey so far. I'm excited to mentor and guide her in the direction she deserves to go in. I'm so grateful that she entered my life.

The true friends are the ones who choose to take a journey with you wherever you go, even when you have not welcomed them.

We all change as time passes.

We grow to be different people, and often it's the hardest for a friend to accept.

We choose different goals and take different paths.

We agree and disagree.

We come to a point where what used to be "fun" is no longer even funny.

What used to be the "time of our lives" becomes time miserably spent today.

We share experiences from the past that we no longer have the desire to experience.

Long conversations become silence.

The moments that seem to be perfect become imperfections.

Losing friends as we learn and grow is easy. However, when we acknowledge that change doesn't mean we have to let go of old friendships, we can be our best selves while remaining in the lives of the people we love. We can fight to stay, and God will bless us with bonds that are everlasting.

We never know the ultimate potential of the people around us. Walking away because we are on different paths may lead us to lose someone who provided support and love in our lives. We must always remind ourselves that just as we are on our journeys of growth, so are our friends.

For me, I've had friendships that will last a lifetime. My true friends were there for me when I had nothing to offer. There were people who stood by my side when I wanted them to leave. They didn't mind helping me to carry my pain. I dug a hole when I was in a dark place, and brought my friends with me. They always had a choice - to leave or to stay - and they chose to stay with me. Now that I live in the light, every success I have is a success we achieved together.

This book has been my own journey of healing, and I owe it to the friends who supported me to get them out of the hole I dug for myself and into the sunshine of my life today.

My success today is just the beginning!

Chapter 42

My Hope for this Book

I hope this book inspires millions, if not billions of people across the globe. I hope this book helps you as the reader heal, like the process of writing it did for me. I want people to know that any story, big or small, is something to be proud of. I want people to not be ashamed to share who they are with the world. It took me years to feel vulnerable enough, to find the courage, to share my story.

Then, I finally understood that I needed to give myself a chance to become who I wanted to become. I had to fight for opportunities that were not just handed out. I had to make decisions and be willing to pay the price. I had to forgive myself and others for my pain in order to start growing. Every chapter of my life brought me closer to who I am today. I truly believe that now. I fell down time and time again, but always got up. Now, I know I will never go back. I refuse to do it, no matter how tired or disappointed I may feel in a given moment. I will continue to work toward transformation because I want my life to impact as many others as possible.

I want to encourage you again now, as you read my story, don't ever focus on failure. Counting every setback as a set up. Get back up, because it is how many times you get up that counts.

Don't be afraid to speak your truth. Your story might inspire someone who is truly in need. These days, I find myself as a mother and a friend, creating job opportunities for others. I am a mentor to people who need empowerment. I am a real estate investor, and now, finally, a proud author who can bring value to so many lives.

As you have learned, I never had a problem turning a page in my life and moving to the next thing. So please, take this from me: Make your amendments, forgive, and move forward to work on your life. Be the best version of you that you possibly can be, and remember, only you know what that version is.

Don't live your life as a victim, and don't give anyone else permission to make you feel like you're not the main character of your own life. When you are afraid of the unknown, when you are afraid of taking chances, decide to take a step towards change. Just make a choice; you can figure out the rest later.

You will realize that venturing into the unknown is when the true magic happens. That's when you can say you've truly lived.

Memories fade too soon, time flies by us too quickly, and even if we could turn back the clock, we'd probably repeat the same stories because they were meant for us. If we work to live as much as possible within the one life we have, we will meet so many different people who impact us in the most incredible ways.

We all walk beside our fellow humans every day, not recognizing each other's unique circumstances in life. We judge people without knowing their stories of life, but deep down, we all share the same spirit.

We each hold a spirit of forgiveness and grace, of humility and care. We just need to dig down deep to uncover our true soul. In the end, the only reason we can feel such profound pain in life is because we were given such profound blessings.

We might feel sad, discouraged, depressed now, but the truth of the matter is that we are so lucky to be able to turn the page. How fortunate we are today to be able to have all of our experiences in life. We get to live stories that change our trajectories forever. We are blessed to live stories that we can share with pride, despite the ugly truth within them.

My scars tell a story. They serve to remind me of times in my life when I was tested. They remind me of the instances where life itself itself tried to break me over and over again,but failed.

My scars serve as a reminder of my repeated trips to dark places, and now they can remind everyone else that darkness is not infinite. Regardless of how much I believed carrying our pain was strength, I had to realize that letting go and embracing peace was my true strength in the end. There is a light at the end of every tunnel, even if it has to come from within you.

Everyone has a story to tell, and every story should be heard. From the stories of others, we can learn that life happens in small bits and in human connection, and that we all have a path to greatness waiting for us.

> "Whatever you're not changing in life, you're choosing."

I encourage you today to take a look at your life and remind yourself of the people - despite their flaws - who brought value to you. Remember the people who gave you their time, because that is the greatest gift someone could ever give. At times, we have to prioritize our goals and dreams, but never forget the people who gave you a helping hand along the way.

I am where I am today in my career and personal life because of my kindness, humility, and forgiveness. However, I am also successful today because of the friendships I have built - the ones that will last a lifetime.

Chapter 43

Special Thank-you

I want to say a big thank-you to all the clients I've had over my years for their loyalty, belief in my work, and contribution to my growth. Because of them, I have confidence in the skills necessary for my career's success today.

I want to thank everyone who has been a part of my journey along the way. Those in my past who have helped shape me, I am grateful for you. However, my future holds space for only a few. The people who enter my life from now on will add to my growth as a human being, personally and professionally, and I am very thankful for that as well.

I dedicate the poem below to those of you - you know exactly who you are - who are in my life today. I will forever be grateful for being blessed with your presence as a part of my story!

"Some people come into our lives and some people go, some move us in directions we can't even imagine, some awaken us to new understandings and new horizons, new dreams we couldn't dream of on our own.

Miracles in life are friendships.

They give us peace in our hearts and calmness in our minds.

They turn our tears into smiles, bringing comfort to the uncomfortable.

They give courage when we are scared, confidence when we are in doubt, faith when we don't believe, and happiness when we feel nothing but sadness.

The happiness friendship brings us always gives us a special lift, and that's how we know that true friendship is one of life's most precious gifts!" - Agnieszka Sycewicz

Chapter 44

Heal Your Past

The process of discovering ourselves can take a lifetime. No matter how many times we transform and restore our lives, we never truly know everything there is to know about who we are. I took a lot of losses to be where I am today, some of those I chose. I still don't understand all of the decisions I've made in life, but maybe that's the point. Everything reveals its reason at some point, even if it isn't immediate.

They say it's lonely at the top. I say it's even lonelier at the bottom. I was often asked if I would die for my kids. When that's the question, my answer would always be a loud and resounding, "YES."

Today though, I believe I did more than that. I didn't die for my kids, but I did survive for them. To me and in my situation, dying would be the easy way out.

"If you dance with the devil long enough you'll get to meet him." Instead of meeting him, I simply decided to stop dancing. For me, choosing God has helped me in every situation, and I will keep choosing Him for the rest of my life. Without Him, I am confident

I would not be in the position I am today. That is the purest truth I know.

Everything we do in this life forces us to choose between good and bad, though it hardly ever seems that black and white. While we know what the difference is in these situations, the real question to help us choose is: What is the price I am willing to pay? Think about it. Is it the price of comfort for what is known, or the price of hardships for what is unknown? Is it the price of being a victim, or chasing victory? The choice, ultimately, is always yours to make.

Everything I have gotten up to this point, I have earned. I used to consider myself a victim, but I don't anymore. However, I don't see myself as a survivor either; I see myself as a warrior, battling in a war I choose to fight.

When we are free to leave hell and we decide to stay, that's when we have been defeated without even knowing we had a choice. The we hold blame for others becomes denial, and we choose to believe it so we can survive. This book illustrates many of my moments of hell, along with many of my moments of heaven. Somehow, I am grateful to the moments from both lives, because they have shaped me.

I have realized that we need to be grateful when we finally meet the devil, because that tells us something important: either we have reached the end of our journey, or it's time to keep fighting so we can reach God. When you give faith a fighting chance, you never have to reach the end. There is always more fighting to do, more good that can enter our lives. When you give faith a fighting chance, what is left is never-ending possibility, opportunity, humility, and love.

I believe "bad" choices come from a place of low self-esteem and insecurity, which we struggle to overcome throughout life. The temporary numbness we choose to place within ourselves when we are feeling low puts us in the position to make choices that do not align with the people we want to be. If we can find confidence and embrace the feelings of life, we have new chances to create realities that match our dreams.

> "To every door that closed on me: I'm coming back to buy the building." - Unknown

There are many levels of healing that we don't realize, and I will share them with you soon. The process I will share with you is the one I followed, and it changed my life forever. It might not make a lot of sense to you at first, but continue until the end. You will heal your past hurt and restore yourself with beautiful memories. We must choose to be soldiers rather than victims, accepting that we sign ourselves up to fight in this war not to survive, but to win. We don't aim to come out alive; we aim to come out victorious.

Sometimes we can bloom in the darkness, if we understand the idea that not every flower blooms in the sunshine. Some do best in the shadows, some can prosper no matter the conditions around them.

We all have a goal that requires hustling, but few are willing to suffer in order to be successful. Adjusting to a new reality takes time, and it's a long process to achieve our dreams. Understanding that notion is the first step toward greatness; willingness is the second.

If you redid your life and deleted the ugly moments, you wouldn't be the same. Those moments are what made your life what it is today.

> "No person is your friend who demands your silence, or denies your right to grow." - Alice Walker

Move on from disappointment, ignore your inner punishment, seek perspective on your limitations and self doubt, connect with people in your life who see your worth even at your worst. Have clarity about where you're heading. Allow others to be different, acknowledge all of the uncomfortable parts of yourself, love and be loved. Decide today to change the changeable, accept the unchangeable, and remove yourself from the unacceptable.

Pause, go back, rethink, recharge, and remember your past as victory, even if sometimes, you feel like you lost. When you fight with faith, you will always come out on top.

Today, follow these simple steps for victory. No matter where you find yourself currently, we will carry the triumph together!

1. Stage One: Denial

We all start with denial. Though we may not be aware of it, it comes in different forms.

A. Denial of denial- When we convince ourselves that we are not experiencing denial.

B. Denial of cycle - An inability to acknowledge what happened to us and a continuation of our harmful patterns as a result

C. Denial of responsibility - The failure to recognize our culpability in an event that we see as being wholly caused by someone else. We claim and believe that what happened to us was someone else's responsibility.

> "If anyone wishes to come after Me, he must deny himself and take up his cross and follow Me." - Matthew 16:24

Denial occurs in our lives because we are secretly afraid to face reality.

It's a well-known human defense mechanism that we adopt quite often, as we focus on protecting our emotions from painful experiences that are difficult for us to accept. Denial is a refusal of accepting reality, and it's often caused by anxiety, insecurity, and fear.

The answer to overcome Denial is to accept what or who we lost during our painful experience.

2. Stage Two: Grief

Grief is the sharpest sorrow in our souls. It's an overwhelming and strong emotional response to great loss that keeps us in mental distress and suffering of painful regrets. Deep down, grief is a powerful feeling that calls us to go back to a certain person we lost or a certain situation that has ended. It's a stage that has no set healing time. In order to move past grief, we must celebrate the positive memories we have surrounding a person or situation.

> "What we once enjoyed and deeply loved we can never lose, for all that we love deeply becomes a part of us." - Helen Keller

3. Stage Three: Anger

Anger is a response in our nervous system that prepares us to fight. It can be good and bad. It can be motivation, or a solution, or a tragedy. Anger is an uncomfortable feeling, and sometimes we feel like we are losing control or patience. Anger can come from frustrations, unfairness, or not feeling appreciated, and it results in a choice of action that works faster than our minds.

> "Anger is the punishment we give ourselves for someone else's mistake." - Gautama Buddha

The answer to healing from anger for me personally was to turn my anger into motivation and success.

4. Stage Four: Depression

Depression appears in our lives when we lose our self worth. It's when we feel doubt, instability, and the highs and lows of our stories. These create an imbalance in our brains, which causes us to feel unworthy, useless, and hopeless. They lower our spirit and capture our emotions, and as a result, we are taken to dark places. We struggle to understand our situations and feel great despair. For some people, the depression can become severe, leading to thoughts of physical harm or suicide. It's one of the most dangerous stages, because it can lead to quick decisions that we might forever regret.

The answer to overcoming this stage is to shift our way of living, to create routines that help build self-confidence. Ways out of depression include surrounding ourselves with positive environments and with positive people, while avoiding loneliness and isolation. We feel less doubtful and more worthy when we push ourselves to create habits that will reward us in the future.

"Depression is living in a body that fights to survive, but with a mind that tries to die." - Anonymous

5. Stage Five: Acceptance

Acceptance is the stage we reach when we don't see our struggles as struggles anymore. The "struggle" is gone; the pain no longer exists because we have admitted our defeat.

Acceptance means we have embraced our pain and our circumstances. We no longer try to defend ourselves or fight against what has occurred. We have learned to tolerate differences and diversity in others, without seeing the need to suffer, and we no longer evaluate or question the memories or situations that became part of our past. We finally recognize reality without trying to change it. In this very final stage, we have let go and are detached from wanting the past to be different.

To gain acceptance, I ask you to focus on your strengths, not your weaknesses. Remind yourself everyday of the gift you have been given. You have been given the ability to overcome phases of your life that once took over your mind. Today, you are ready. You are on the path to healing, to living the magical life you are about to create!

"True happiness can only exist with acceptance."

When I look back on my journey, I can see now that I needed to rescue myself before I could rescue anybody else. I needed to heal in order to help others heal. I first started writing this book with the goal of sharing my story. I wanted to inspire people around the world to believe in themselves, to believe they could be the heroes in their own lives

As much as I felt healed before embarking on this journey, I didn't realize how much pain I still carried with me. Revisiting the moments that created a lasting impact on my life brought a lot of tears. I shared the stories with you, andI kept writing - sometimes I think with more pain than I felt when the events initially occurred. I almost gave up at different points along the way; I didn't think

I could experience any more pain than I already had. Writing this book opened up wounds I had long assumed were healed.

Without knowing it, this journey of writing has helped to heal deep wounds that were buried, covered with temporary numbness. I read each chapter over and over again throughout the process, discovering many emotions I didn't know existed. I have continued putting my feelings on empty pages. As I went back through my writing, the tears varied from strong downpours to steady drizzles. Eventually, there were no tears left. To me, that represented my recovery - the healing of the broken person I wasn't aware was still inside. That was a magical moment in my life. Now, I know I'm healed!

Chapter 45

Healing Process

Exercise

People often say, "time heals all wounds." I disagree. Our wounds can last a lifetime if we do not choose to confront and heal from them, but there is hope. I encourage everyone who may be struggling with healing to follow the steps I have outlined here. Try out this process and watch the magic happen in your life! Wounded Memories Healing Process - Healing your past lives and characters

Empty pages are really the only material you will need. I want you to focus on one story at a time, one journey of healing at a time. All of our healing is connected, yes, but each event that has caused pain is also uniquely its own. For this exercise, you will be going back in time to the very first tragedy you can remember, or what you consider the first painful time in your life.

As you record your memories, don't forget to write the feelings you were experiencing in that very moment. This process will force you to experience many emotions you don't want to face. Depending on who you are, you may feel like you're drowning in your own tears. Don't stop. Keep sharing your thoughts with those empty pages. Write and write, until you think that chapter has ended. Read your story out loud, and you might find yourself adding or deleting details that better align with the truth you believe in.When you're ready, go back and read your memory again, repeating this process of adding and subtracting information from your story to match your beliefs. Throughout this exercise, your emotions may range from suffering, to pain, to deep sadness and grief, to forgiveness, to acceptance, to finally remarkable and extreme happiness and freedom. If you find yourself shedding tears, you will know you are moving toward healing when you have no more tears to spare. When you reach that moment, when you are no longer crying or feeling hurt over the past, get another blank page and answer the questions laid out further down in the Five Stages of Healing. After that, take some time, and once you're ready, write another chapter of pain and repeat the process.

> "Whatever burden you are facing isn't accidental and will never be." - Unknown

The questions below will allow you to understand the person you are today because of your moments of pain. Answer them based on that person - the person you are today, the one who has a new wealth of growth and life experience behind them - rather than the person you once were. In this way, the overall goal is to figure out who you are so you can live your life to the fullest potential with every blessing and new beginning that is meant for you.

Use this guide as an approach for recovery toward full healing:

1. Denial

Who did I lose?
What did I lose at this moment?
What was my choice?
What was my consequence?
What was my lesson learned in this event?
Whose responsibility is it during the moment of blame?
Would I erase this person or situation from my life, knowing the outcome?

2. Grief

What was the happy memory about the person or event?
What can you celebrate about this situation?
What caused you to suffer?
What was the reason for the pain you experienced?
What is the hardest part to forget?
If you could choose to forget or forgive, what choice would you make?

3. Anger

Why was I angry?
Who was I angry with?
What triggered the anger inside me?
What could I have done differently?
What was the main moment of anger?
Was it a person or a situation that caused the anger?
Admit your mistake.
What was my reality when I was angry?

4. Depression

Did I feel unworthy?
What feeling did I lose during that moment?
Did I give up?
What scene allowed me to give up?
Did I consider myself a victim?
Name three things the person who caused you pain did that made you feel a lack of self esteem.

5. Acceptance

What made me feel empty?
What was the reason for faith in that moment?
Why did I decide to grow?
What was my emotional need in my time of tragedy?
Why did I choose to go back to my past?

Am I a survivor or a victim?
Do I consider myself a warrior?
Do I forgive?
Why do I forgive this person?
Why do I forgive myself?

When you are done answering these questions, put your answers in sentences. Read them out loud as many times as you can, until you no longer feel the pain of regret or have tears to spare.

> "Healing takes courage, and we all have courage, even if we have to dig a little to find it." - Tori Amos

"Healing within"

ABOUT THE AUTHOR

Agnieszka Sycewicz has proven to be successful along her journey, transitioning from a rebellious, poor teenager from a foreign country to a notable female entrepreneur. She is also a single mother of three teenage boys, and currently resides in Hollywood, Florida.

Agnieszka is a sport massage therapist, helping people around the world. She is the CEO of LIONESSEMPIRE.LLC, a mobile massage company in Florida that is expanding to New York City. She is also a real estate investor in Florida, whose focus is fixing and flipping single-family homes.

Agnieszka is also an author; her knowledge and kind heart help to bring those around her to new, higher levels of growth along with her. Dreaming and striving for greatness has been a way of life for her, as she took every chance she could to make it where she is today. She often likes to quote the title of this book, "Give faith a fighting chance," as it has proven true in her own life time and time again.

She spends her free time with loved ones and travels the world.

Agnieszka is a community builder, as well as a mentor, to those who struggle with their past and are in need of a life change. She is a woman of excellence; she has no fear. If you ask her, her success is only just beginning!

Agnieszka can be found on social media:

@Agnieszkasycewicz
@massagetherapy_empire
@agnimilestone_investor

www.ingramcontent.com/pod-product-compliance
Lightning Source LLC
Chambersburg PA
CBHW050110170426
43198CB00014B/2515